Sermon Classics by
Great Preachers

Sermon Classics by Great Preachers

compiled by

Peter F. Gunther

MOODY PRESS

CHICAGO

Revised Edition

ISBN: 0-8024-3328-6

Library of Congress Cataloging in Publication Data
Main entry under title:

Sermons Classics by Great Preachers.

Rev. ed. of: Great Sermons by Great Preachers. [1960]
Contents: The Fire Sermon/Dwight Lyman Moody—Sinners in the Hands of an Angry God/Jonathan Edwards—The Most Wonderful Sentence ever written/ Reuben Archer Torrey—[etc.]
1. Sermons, English. I. Gunther, Peter F.
BV4241.S414 1982   252   81-16899
ISBN 0-8024-3328-6   AACR2

2 3 4 5 6 7 Printing/LC/Year 87 86 85 84 83 82

PRINTED IN THE UNITED STATES OF AMERICA

CONTENTS

65436

THE FIRE SERMON

Dwight Lyman Moody

(1837-1899)

On Sunday night, October 8, 1871, Dwight L. Moody was preaching to a large congregation in Farwell Hall in Chicago. It was the fifth of a series of six sermons on the life of Christ. He proposed to preach the sixth and the last of the series on the following Sunday. The courthouse bell was sounding an alarm of fire, but he paid no attention to it. The people were accustomed to hearing the fire bell, and it did not disturb them much when it sounded. He finished his sermon on "What Shall I Do with Jesus?" and said to the audience:

"Now, I want you to take the question with you and think it over, and next Sunday I want you to come back and tell me what you are going to do with Him."

In a short time that congregation was a crowd of wildly fleeing fugitives, and their homes and Farwell Hall were heaps of smoking ruins.

Twenty-two years later Chicago celebrated the anniversary of that fire on a large scale, hoping to draw the largest number of people to the World's Fair by having a "Chicago Day." Mr. Moody resolved to take advantage of the circumstances to make October 8, 1893, a great day for the cause of Jesus Christ. Arrangements were made for an extraordinary meeting in the central Music Hall running from 10:00 A.M. to 2:30 P.M. One part of the service was to be a repetition by Mr. Moody of the sermon he had preached on the night of the fire twenty-two years before.

The hall was filled, with hundreds of disappointed people outside vainly trying to gain entrance. The meeting went on uninterrupted for the four and one-half hours, closing with Mr. Moody's sermon the last half hour.

THE FIRE SERMON

IN THE SPRING OF '71, along with Philip Phillips and Reverend (now Bishop) J. H. Vincent, I went to California, and when I came back to Chicago hot weather had come, and our audience had become scattered. I came to Farwell Hall, wanting to get back the audience, but nearly all had gone, and it seemed almost impossible to get them together again. I remember that for a number of weeks I was turning over in my mind what to do to accomplish that. I thought I would plan some kind of sacred concerts or get someone to lecture on historical events, for I thought that the gospel would not draw.

But I remember that after praying over it and getting up from my knees the thought came to me, *Preach to them on Bible characters.* Well, I had some six or eight Bible characters in mind, and I thought I would try Adam first. So I took Adam and looked him over, but I thought I could never talk about him for thirty minutes. Then I thought I would try Enoch. I think I took up Noah next, and I came to Abraham and had him as one of the characters. I advertised that I would speak so many nights on the Bible characters. It was not long before Farwell Hall began to fill up, and in five weeks I had the largest congregations I had ever spoken to in Chicago.

I intended to devote six nights to Christ's life. I had spent four Sunday nights on the subject, and had followed Him from the manger along through His life to His arrest and trial, and on the fifth Sunday night, October 8, I was preaching to the largest congregation I had ever had in Chicago, quite elated with my success. My text was, "What shall I do then with Jesus which is called the Christ?" That night I made one of the greatest mistakes of my life. After preaching—or talking, as I did not call it preaching then—with all the power that God had given me, urging Christ upon the people, I closed the sermon and said, "I wish you would take this text home with you and turn it over in your minds during the week, and next Sunday we will come to Calvary and the cross, and we will decide what we will do with Jesus of Nazareth."

I have never seen that congregation since. I have hard work to keep back the tears today. I have looked over this audience, and not a single one is here that I preached to that night. I have a great many old friends and am pretty well acquainted in Chicago, but twenty-two years have passed away, and I have not seen that congregation since, and I

9

will never meet those people again until I meet them in another world. But I want to tell you one lesson I learned that night, which I have never forgotten, and that is, when I preach to press Christ upon the people then and there, I try to bring them to a decision on the spot. I would rather have that right hand cut off than give an audience a week to decide what to do with Jesus.

I have often been criticized, and people have said: "Moody, you seem to try to get people to decide all at once. Why do you not give them time to consider?" I have asked God many times to forgive me for telling people that night to take a week to think it over, and if He spares my life I will never do it again. This audience will break up in a few moments, and we will never meet again. There is something awfully solemn about a congregation like this!

You will notice that Pilate was just in the condition that my audience was that night, just the condition that you are in here today—he had to decide then and there what to do with Jesus. The thing was sprung upon him suddenly, although I do not think that Jesus Christ could have been a stranger to Pilate. I do not believe that He had preached in Judea for months, and also in Jerusalem, without Pilate hearing of His teaching. He must have heard of the sermons He had preached; he must have heard of the doctrines He taught; he must have heard of the wonderful parables that He uttered; he must have heard about the wonderful miracles that He had performed; he must have heard how Herod had taken the life of His forerunner by having him beheaded, and of the cruel way he had treated Him, so that he was no stranger to Jesus of Nazareth.

The Fire Sermon

But I do not believe that there is a child here today that has not a better knowledge of Christ than Pilate had. We have had more than eighteen hundred years of gospel proclamation in this dark world and have seen the fruits of Christianity as Pilate never did. He never had seen Christ in His glorified state. The only time he saw Him was in His humiliation, despised and rejected of men. The chief men that followed Christ were men of no account, men of no power, of no title, of no influence, of no position or culture. There was no crown on His brow except the crown of thorns, no scepter in His hand except the reed placed there in derision and mockery.

But we have seen Christ glorified, and we see Him today by the throne of God. We have far more light than Pilate had, and yet Pilate had his day; and I believe every man and woman have their day of opportunity. That was Pilate's day. The Son of God crossed his path that day, and he was exalted to Heaven with privilege. It was a glorious privilege that he had. If he had decided according to his own conscience, even according to his own deceitful heart, and had been influenced by his wife, Pilate might have been immortal. He might have had his name associated with that of Joseph of Arimathea, with the twelve disciples of the Lamb, and with those foremost to herald the name of Jesus, if he had only acted according to his conscience. But there was another influence about him. The world came in; political preferment came in; the Roman government came in, and he wanted to win the favor of the Caesars. There you see that weak, vacillating man in the balance, wavering. Hear his decision: "I find no fault in him."

11

Did you ever notice that God makes all His enemies testify that Jesus is the Son of God? The centurion who had charge of His execution smote his breast and said: "Certainly this was a righteous man." And Judas, after having betrayed the Son of God, said: "I have betrayed innocent blood." And Pilate had to testify that he could find no fault in Him.

I do not believe that ever in the history of the world was there a more unjust judgment given than that of Pilate on Jesus Christ. After examination he declared, "I find no fault in this man," and in the same breath he said, "I will chastise Him."

The process of scourging was very cruel. They took the prisoner, bound his wrists, and fastened him in a stooping posture, and the scourge, which is made of cord knotted with sharp pieces of steel, was brought down upon the bare back of the victim, lacerating the flesh, cutting it to the bone, and many a man died under the infliction.

Pilate scourged an innocent Man, but he wanted to curry favor with the Jews and also hold with the Romans, and that was his decision. The Jews had the judge. They saw he was vacillating and knew he was the man for them, and that they could get their own way. They said: "If you let that man go you are not Caesar's friend." Then he tried to shift the responsibility. What man is there here who has not tried to shift responsibility in the same way? And I tell you that every one of you will have to decide for himself what he will do with Jesus. Your wife cannot decide it for you; no friend on earth can decide for you.

It was the custom to release a prisoner at the feast of the Passover, so Pilate took the most noted criminal he had and asked the people whether he should release Barabbas or Christ. He thought they would rather have Christ than Barabbas, but they cried out: "Barabbas! Barabbas!" Then Pilate asked: "What shall I do then with Jesus, who is called the Christ?" He had sent Him to Herod, but Herod had sent Him back and refused to take His life. And when Pilate found that he could not prevail, he was willing to go with the multitude instead of standing up against the current.

What we want in this city is men to stand up for the right; and even if you do suffer for a little while, the crowning day is coming. We want men to stand up against the current, not go with it, and not only to stand up against the current, but to go right against it. There was Pilate's failure.

Hardly any name in history shines brighter than that of Joseph of Arimathea. I can imagine him that night in the council chamber when Jesus was condemned by the Sanhedrin. "What think ye?" Is the question. And then it rang out through the judgment hall, "He is guilty of death!" But away down at the other end of the hall Joseph arose, and with a clear, ringing voice he said: "I will never give my consent to that just Man's death!" How that voice must have refreshed the soul of the Son of God in that dark night, when not one stood by Him, when all cried out against Him! Oh, it is an honor to confess Christ!

There never will be a time when we can do more for Christ than now, and there is no better place than here in Chicago. May God help us to take our stand in these dark days when Christ is rejected by so many and when they are telling us that He is not the Savior of the world and are putting Him on a level with other men. Come out and take a high stand for Christ. Let others go on scoffing, but you come out and identify yourself with the disciples of Jesus Christ. Take a high stand—that is what we want to do. May God help you!

Pilate had come to the fork in the road. That was a memorable day in his history, for he had only to take the advice of his wife and obey his conscience. She had sent word to him, saying, "Have thou nothing to do with that just man; for I have suffered many things this day in a dream because of him." It may be that God warns you sometimes in dreams. He evidently did warn Pilate through the dream of his wife.

I was reading not long ago of a mother who had a daughter who was away from home visiting with friends. She dreamed that her daughter was murdered and buried under the barn floor. The dream made such an impression on her that she had the barn floor taken up, and there was the daughter just as she had dreamed.

I do not know what Pilate's wife's dream was, but perhaps she had a dream of the judgment day, and saw Christ sitting upon a throne with the angels about Him, and Pilate coming before Him to be judged, and she was terrified and made haste and sent word to her husband: "Have nothing to do with that just man; for I have suffered many things this day in a dream because of him." Every man who had anything to do with the murder of Christ soon came to a terrible end. Be careful about your decision in regard to Jesus, for He is to be the judge of the world.

I cannot detain you much longer, but I would like today to press upon you this one question: "What shall I do with Jesus Christ?" I cannot speak for the rest of you, but ever since that night of the great fire I have determined as long as God spares my life to make more of Christ than in the past. I thank God that He is a thousand times more to me today than He was twenty-two years ago ... I made some vows after that Chicago fire, and I want to tell you that God has helped me to keep those vows. I am not what I wish I were, but I am a better man than I was when Chicago was on fire.

As I was preparing to leave London the last time I was there, I called on a celebrated physician who told me my heart was weakening and that I had to let up on my work, that I had to be more careful of myself; and I was going home with the thought that I would not work quite so hard.

I was on that ill-fated steamer the *Spree* when the announcement came that the vessel was sinking and that there was no hope. The stern had sunk thirty feet, and we were there forty-eight hours in that helpless condition. No one on earth knew what I passed through during those hours, as I thought that my work was finished, that I would never again have the privilege of preaching the gospel of the Son of God. And on that dark night, the first night of the accident, I made a vow that if God would spare my life and bring me back to America, I would come back to Chicago and at this World's Fair preach the gospel with all the power that He would give me; and God has enabled me to keep that vow during the past five months. It seems as if I went to the very gates of heaven during those forty-eight hours on the sinking ship, and God permitted me to come back and preach Christ a little longer.

And I would like to say that if there is a man or woman in this house today living under a broken vow, you had better right here and now, in the presence of these people, resolve to pay your vows before God.

Sometimes we wait for a calamity to strike us. When the Chicago fire struck me I was in middle life—if I live out the time allotted to man. After the first I just looked around, and I cannot tell you what a blessing that fire was to me. I think when calamity comes we ought to get all we can out of it, and if God has a lesson for us to learn, let us take the lesson. It may be that God has a wonderful lesson for us. I will venture to say that many of you here have been in this same state. You that are in middle life, look around and ask yourself whether your life is what it ought to be. Come today for a little review, and look down along the way from whence you came. Do you not see some spot in your life where you have made a vow and have not kept it? You have said, "I will be a more consecrated man, or I will be a Christian"; you have stood by the bedside of a dying mother and have said, "I will meet you in the better world."

Are you going to make good that promise? Why not do so here, just at the close of this four-hour meeting? Make up your minds that you will carry out that vow. It may be I am talking to a father or mother who has laid away a little child. When that child was taken away you said: "I am going to live a more consecrated life; I will not get rooted and grounded in things below, but I will rather set my affections on things above; I will make good my vow."

It is only a little while, a few months, a few years,

and we will all be gone. May God help us now to pay our vows in the presence of all the people. Come now, while I am speaking, and make a full, complete, and unconditional surrender to God, and say, "Here am I, Lord; take me and use me; let me have the privilege of being a co-worker with Thee," and there will be a fire kindled here that will burn into eternity. This hour, this minute, make up your minds that you are going to be from this time forth on the Lord's side. Go to your home, to your church, and give a ringing testimony for the Son of God. Go to work, do what you can for Christ, and there will be grand days for this republic and a blessed life for you here and hereafter.

With this closing appeal Moody turned to God with a fervent prayer of thanksgiving, consecration, supplication, and tearful intercession for the city and for the multitudes coming to the fair. Then once more the people united in singing, and were dismissed with benediction, to meet again no more until all the earth shall stand before the judgment seat of Christ.

SINNERS IN THE HANDS
OF AN ANGRY GOD

Jonathan Edwards

(1703-1758)

This sermon was preached on the afternoon of July 8, 1741, in Enfield, Connecticut. Revival fires had been started throughout the New England area by George Whitefield, but Enfield, the most wicked community of them all, had not been moved. A special service had been called by a group of ministers with Jonathan Edwards as the speaker for the afternoon session. As the ministers entered the meeting place, they were shocked by the levity of the congregation. They appeared thoughtless and vain and hardly conducted themselves with common decency.

As Edwards preached, he used no gestures but stood motionless. His left elbow leaned on the pulpit and his left hand held his notes. His text was Deuteronomy 32:35, "Their foot shall slide in due time."

Probably no sermon has ever had the effect of this one. It was interrupted by outcries from the congregation—men and women stood up and rolled on the floor, their cries once drowning out the voice of the preacher. Some are said to have laid hold on the pillars and braces of the church, apparently feeling that at that very moment their feet were sliding, that they were being precipitated into hell. All through the house one could hear the cries of those feeling themselves lost, crying to God for mercy.

Through the night Enfield was like a beleaguered city. In almost every house men and women could be heard crying out for God to save them.

SINNERS IN THE HANDS
OF AN ANGRY GOD

Their foot shall slide in due time
(Deuteronomy 32:35).

IN THIS VERSE the vengeance of God is threatened on the wicked, unbelieving Israelites who were God's visible people and who lived under means of grace. Notwithstanding all God's wonderful works that He had wrought toward that people, they remained, as expressed in verse 28, void of counsel, having no understanding in them; and that, under all the cultivations of heaven, brought forth bitter and poisonous fruit as in the two verses preceding the text.

The expression that I have chosen for my text, "Their foot shall slide in due time," seems to imply the following things relating to the punishment and destruction that those wicked Israelites were exposed to.

1. That they were always exposed to destruction, as one that stands or walks in slippery places is always exposed to fall. This is implied in the manner

of their destruction's coming upon them, being represented by their foot's sliding. The same is expressed in Psalm 73:18: "Surely thou didst set them in slippery places: thou castedst them down into destruction."

2. It implies that they were always exposed to *sudden*, unexpected destruction. As he that walks in slippery places is every moment liable to fall, he cannot foresee one moment whether he shall stand or fall the next; and when he does fall, he falls at once, without warning, which is also expressed in Psalm 73:18-19: "Surely thou didst set them in slippery places: thou castedst them down into de struction. How are they brought into desolation, as *in a moment!*"

3. Another thing implied is that they are liable to fall of *themselves*, without being thrown down by the hand of another; as he that stands or walks on slippery ground needs nothing but his own weight to throw him down.

4. That the reason why they are not fallen already, and do not fall now, is only that God's appointed time is not come. For it is said that when that due time, or appointed time, comes, *their foot shall slide.* Then they shall be left to fall, as they are inclined by their own weight. God will not hold them up in these slippery places any longer, but will let them go; and then, at that very instant, they shall fall to destruction. As he that stands in such slippery declining ground on the edge of a pit that he cannot stand alone, when he is let go he immediately falls and is lost.

The observation from the words that I would now insist upon is this,

"There is nothing that keeps wicked men at any

one moment out of hell, but the mere pleasure of God."

By the mere pleasure of God I mean His sovereign pleasure, His arbitrary will, restrained by no obligation, hindered by no manner of difficulty, any more than if nothing else but God's mere will had in the least degree or in any respect whatsoever any hand in the preservation of wicked men one moment.

The truth of this observation may appear by the following considerations.

1. There is no want of *power* in God to cast wicked men into hell at any moment. Men's hands cannot be strong when God rises up: the strongest have no power to resist Him, nor can any deliver out of His hands.

He is not only able to cast wicked men into hell, but He can most easily do it. Sometimes an earthly prince meets with a great deal of difficulty to subdue a rebel that has found means to fortify himself and has made himself strong by the number of his followers. But it is not so with God. There is no fortress that is any defense against the power of God. Though hand join in hand, and vast multitudes of God's enemies combine and associate themselves, they are easily broken in pieces. They are as great heaps of light chaff before the whirlwind or large quantities of dry stubble before devouring flames. We find it easy to tread on and crush a worm that we see crawling on the earth. So it is easy for us to cut or singe a slender thread that anything hangs by; thus easy is it for God, when He pleases, to cast His enemies down to hell. What are we, that we should think to stand before Him, at whose rebuke the earth trembles, and before whom the rocks are thrown down.

2. They *deserve* to be cast into hell. So that divine justice never stands in the way, it makes no objection against God's using His power at any moment to destroy them. Yea, on the contrary, justice calls aloud for an infinite punishment of their sins. Divine justice says of the tree that brings forth such grapes of Sodom: "Cut it down, why cumbereth it the ground?" (Luke 13:7). The sword of divine justice is every moment brandished over their heads, and it is nothing but the hand of arbitrary mercy and God's mere will that holds it back.

3. They are *already* under a sentence of condemnation to hell. They not only justly deserve to be cast down thither, but the sentence of the law of God, that eternal and immutable rule of righteousness that God has fixed between Him and mankind, is gone out against them, and stands against them; so that they are bound over already to hell. "He that believeth not is condemned already" (John 3:18). So that every unconverted man properly belongs to hell; that is his place; from thence he is. "Ye are from beneath" (John 8:23); and thither he is bound. It is the place that justice, and God's Word, and the sentence of His unchangeable law, assigns to him.

4. They are now the objects of that very *same* anger and wrath of God that is expressed in the torments of hell. And the reason they do not go down to hell at each moment is not because God, in whose power they are, is not then very angry with them—as angry as He is with many of those miserable creatures He is now tormenting in hell and do there feel and bear the fierceness of His wrath. Yea, God is a great deal more angry with great numbers that are now on earth, yea, doubtless, with

many that are now in this congregation, that, it may be, are at ease and quiet, than He is with many of those that are now in the flames of hell.

It is not because God is unmindful of their wickedness and does not resent it that He does not let loose His hand and cut them off. God is not altogether such a one as themselves, though they may imagine Him to be so. The wrath of God burns against them; their damnation does not slumber; the pit is prepared; the fire is made ready; the furnace is now hot, ready to receive them; the flames do now rage and glow. The glittering sword is whet and held over them, and the pit has opened her mouth under them.

5. The devil stands ready to fall upon them, and seize them as his own, at what moment God shall permit him. They belong to him; he has their souls in his possession, and under his dominion. The Scripture represents them as his *goods* (Luke 11:21). The devils watch them; they are ever by them, at their right hand; they stand waiting for them, like greedy hungry lions that see their prey and expect to have it, but are for the present kept back. If God would withdraw His hand by which they are restrained, they would in one moment fly upon their poor souls. The old serpent is gaping for them. Hell opens its mouth wide to receive them, and if God should permit it, they would be hastily swallowed up and lost.

6. There are in the souls of wicked men those hellish *principles* reigning that would presently kindle and flame out into hell-fire, if it were not for God's restraints. There is laid in the very nature of carnal men a foundation for the torments of hell. There are those corrupt principles, in reigning power

in them, and in full possession of them, that are seeds of hell-fire. These principles are active and powerful, exceedingly violent in their nature, and if it were not for the restraining hand of God upon them, they would soon break out. They would flame out after the same manner as the same corruptions, the same enmity does in the hearts of damned souls, and would beget the same torments in them as they do in them.

The souls of the wicked are compared to the troubled sea (Isaiah 57:20). For the present God restrains their wickedness by His mighty power, as He does the raging waves of the troubled sea, saying, "Hitherto shalt thou come, and no further." But if God should withdraw that restraining power, it would soon carry all before it. Sin is the ruin and misery of the soul; it is destructive in its nature; and if God should leave it without restraint, nothing else would be needed to make the soul perfectly miserable. The corruption of the heart of man is a thing that is immoderate and boundless in its fury. While wicked men live here, it is like fire pent up by God's restraints, when if it were let loose it would set on fire the course of nature. And as the heart is now a sink of sin, so, if sin were not restrained, it would immediately turn the soul into a fiery oven, or a furnace of fire and brimstone.

7. It is no security to wicked men for one moment that there are *no visible means of death* at hand. It is no security to a natural man that he is now in health, and that he does not see how he might go out of the world by any accident, and that there is no visible danger in any respect in his circumstances. The manifold and continual experience of the world in all ages shows that this is no

evidence that a man is not on the very brink of eternity and that the next step will not be into another world. The unseen, unthought of ways and means of persons' going suddenly out of the world are innumerable and inconceivable. Unconverted men walk over the pit of hell on a rotten covering, and there are innumerable places in this covering so weak that they will not bear their weight, and these places are not seen.

The arrows of death fly unseen at noonday; the sharpest sight cannot discern them. God has so many different, unsearchable ways of taking wicked men out of the world and sending them to hell that there is nothing to make it appear that God need be at the expense of a miracle or go out of the ordinary course of His providence to destroy any wicked man at any moment. All the means there are of sinners going out of the world are in God's hands and so absolutely subject to His power and determination, that it does not depend at all less on the mere will of God, whether sinners shall at any moment go to hell, than if means were never made use of, or at all concerned in the case.

8. Natural men's *prudence* and *care* to preserve their own *lives* or the care of others to preserve them, does not secure them a moment. To this, divine providence and universal experience also bear testimony. There is this clear evidence that men's own wisdom is no security to them from death; that if it were otherwise, we should see some difference between the wise and politic men of the world and others, with regard to their liableness to early and unexpected death. But how is it in fact? "How dieth the wise man? as the fool" (Ecclesiastes 2:16).

9. All wicked men's *pains* and the *contrivances* they use to escape *hell,* while they continue to reject Christ and so remain wicked men, does not secure them from hell one moment. Almost every natural man that hears of hell flatters himself that he shall escape it. He depends on himself for his own security; he flatters himself in what he has done, in what he is now doing, or what he intends to do.

Everyone lays out matters in his own mind how he shall avoid damnation and flatters himself that he contrives well for himself and that his schemes will not fail. They hear indeed that there are but few saved, and that the bigger part of men that have died heretofore are gone to hell. But each one imagines that he lays out matters better for his own escape than others have done. He does not intend to come to that place of torment. He says within himself that he intends to take care that shall be effectual and to order matters so for himself as not to fail.

But the foolish children of men miserably delude themselves in their own schemes and in their confidence in their own strength and wisdom; they trust to nothing but a shadow. The bigger part of those that heretofore have lived under the same means of grace, and are now dead, are undoubtedly gone to hell. It was not because they were not as wise as those that are now alive. It was not because they did not lay out matters as well for themselves to secure their own escape. If it were so that we could speak with them and could inquire of them whether they expected when alive, and when they heard about hell ever to be subjects of that misery, we doubtless should hear one and another reply,

"No, I never intended to come here. I had laid

out matters otherwise in my mind. I thought I should contrive well for myself. I thought my scheme good. I intended to take effectual care. But it came upon me unexpected; I did not look for it at that time, and in that manner. It came as a thief; death outwitted me; God's wrath was too quick for me. Oh, my cursed foolishness! I was flattering myself and pleasing myself with vain dreams of what I would do hereafter. When I was saying peace and safety, then sudden destruction came upon me."

10. God has laid Himself under *no obligation*, by any promise, to keep any natural man out of hell one moment. God certainly has made no promises either of eternal life, or of any deliverance or preservation from eternal death, but what are contained in the covenant of grace, the promises that are given in Christ, in whom all the promises are yea and amen. But surely they have no interest in the promises of the covenant of grace that are not the children of the covenant, do not believe in any of the promises of the covenant, and have no interest in the mediator of the covenant.

Whatever some have imagined and pretended about promises made to natural men's earnest seeking and knocking, it is plain and manifest that whatever pains a natural man takes in religion, whatever prayers he makes, till he believes in Christ, God is under no manner of obligaiton to keep him a moment from eternal destruction.

So it is that natural men are held in the hand of God over the pit of hell. They have deserved the fiery pit and are already sentenced to it. God is dreadfully provoked; His anger is as great toward them as toward those that are actually suffering the executions of the fierceness of His wrath in hell, and they have done nothing in the least to appease or abate that anger. Neither is God in the least bound by any promise to hold them up one moment.

The devil is waiting for them; hell is gaping for them; the flames gather and flash about them, and would fain lay hold on them and swallow them up. The fire pent up in their own hearts is struggling to break out. They have no interest in any mediator; there are no means within reach that can be any security to them. In short they have no refuge, nothing to take hold of; all that preserves them every moment is the mere arbitrary will and uncovenanted, unobliged forebearance of an incensed God.

APPLICATION

The use of this awful subject may be for an awakening of unconverted persons to a conviction of their danger. This is the case of every one of you who are out of Christ. That world of misery, that lake of burning brimstone, is extended abroad under you. There is the dreadful pit of the glowing flames of the wrath of God. There is hell's wide gaping mouth open, and you have nothing to stand on, nor anything to take hold of. There is nothing between you and hell but the air; it is only the power and mere pleasure of God that holds you up.

You probably are not conscious of that. You find you are kept out of hell but do not see the hand of God in it. You look at other things, as the good state of your bodily constitution, your care of your own life, and the means you use for your own preservation. But instead those things are nothing. If God should withdraw His hand they would avail no more to keep you from falling than the thin air to hold up a person who is suspended in it.

Your wickedness makes you as it were heavy as lead and to tend downward with great weight and pressure toward hell. If God should let you go, you would immediately sink and swiftly descend and plunge into the bottomless gulf, and your healthy constitution, your own care and prudence, best contrivance, and all your righteousness would have no more influence to uphold you and keep you out of hell than a spider's web would have to stop a falling rock.

Were it not for the sovereign pleasure of God, the earth would not bear you one moment. You are a burden to it; the creation groans with you; the creature is made subject to the bondage of your corruption not willingly. The sun does not willingly shine upon you to give you light to serve sin and Satan. The earth does not willingly yield her increase to satisfy your lusts, nor is it willingly a stage for your wickedness to be acted upon. The air does not willingly serve you for breath to maintain the flame of life in your vitals while you spend your life in the service of God's enemies.

God's creatures are good, were made for men to serve God with, do not willingly subserve to any other purpose, and groan when they are abused to purposes so directly contrary to their nature and end. The world would spew you out, were it not for the sovereign hand of Him who has subjected it in hope. There are the black clouds of God's wrath now hanging directly over your heads, full of the dreadful storm and big with thunder; and were it not for the restraining hand of God it would immediately burst forth upon you. The sovereign pleasure of God, for the present, stays His rough wind. Otherwise it would come with fury, your destruction would come like a whirlwind, and you would be like the chaff of the summer threshing floor.

The wrath of God is like great waters that are damned for the present. They increase more and more and rise higher and higher till an outlet is given. The longer the stream is stopped, the more rapid and mighty is its course when once it is let loose.

It is true that judgment against your evil work has not been executed hitherto; the floods of God's vengeance have been withheld. But your guilt in the meantime is constantly increasing, and you are every day treasuring up more wrath. The waters are continually rising and waxing more and more mighty; and there is nothing but the mere pleasure of God that holds back the waters that are unwilling to be stopped and press hard to go forward.

If God should only withdraw His hand from the floodgate it would immediately fly open, and the fiery floods of the fierceness and wrath of God would rush forth with inconceivable fury and would come upon you with omnipotent power. If your strength were ten thousand times greater than it is, yea, ten thousand times greater than the strength of the stoutest, sturdiest devil in hell, it would be nothing to withstand or endure it.

The bow of God's wrath is bent, and the arrow made ready on the string, and justice bends the arrow at your heart and strains the bow, and it is nothing but the mere pleasure of God, and of an angry God, without any promise or obligation at all, that keeps the arrow one moment from being made drunk with your blood.

Jonathan Edwards

Thus are all you that never passed under a great change of heart by the mighty power of the Spirit of God upon your souls. All that were never born again, made new creatures, and raised from being dead in sin to a state of new, and before altogether unexperienced light and life (however you may have reformed your life in many things, and may have had religious affections, and may keep up a form of religion in your families and closets, and in the house of God, and may be strict in it), you are thus in the hands of an angry God. It is nothing but His mere pleasure that keeps you from being this moment swallowed up in everlasting destruction.

However unconvinced you may now be of the truth of what you hear, by and by you will be fully convinced of it. Those that are gone from being in like circumstances with you see that it was so with them. Destruction came suddenly upon most of them, when they expected nothing of it, and while they were saying, "Peace and safety." Now they see that those things they depended on for peace and safety were nothing but thin air and empty shadows.

The God that holds you over the pit of hell, much as one holds a spider or some loathsome insect over the fire, abhors you and is dreadfully provoked. His wrath toward you burns like fire; He looks upon you as worthy of nothing else but to be cast into the fire. He is of purer eyes than to bear to have you in His sight. You are ten thousand times as abominable in His eyes, as the most hateful and venomous serpent is in ours. You have offended Him infinitely more than ever a stubborn rebel did his prince, and yet it is nothing but His hand that holds you from falling into the fire every moment.

Sinners in the Hands of an Angry God

It is ascribed to nothing else that you did not go to hell last night; that you were suffered to awake again in this world after you closed your eyes to sleep. There is no other reason to be given why you have not dropped into hell since you arose in the morning, but that God's hand has held you up. There is no other reason to be given why you have not gone to hell since you have sat here in the house of God, provoking His pure eyes by your sinful wicked manner of attending His solemn worship. Yea, there is nothing else that is to be given as a reason why you do not this very moment drop down into hell.

Consider the fearful danger you are in! It is a great furnace of wrath, a wide and bottomless pit, full of the fire of wrath, that you are held over in the hand of that God whose wrath is provoked and incensed as much against you as against many of the damned in hell. You hang by a slender thread, with the flames of divine wrath flashing about it and ready every moment to singe it and burn it asunder. You have no interest in any mediator, nothing to lay hold of to save yourself, nothing to keep off the flames of wrath, nothing of your own, nothing that you ever have done, nothing that you can do to induce God to spare you one moment.

And consider here more particularly whose wrath it is. It is the wrath of the infinite God. If it were only the wrath of man, though it were of the most potent prince, it would be comparatively little to be regarded. The wrath of kings is very much dreaded, especially of absolute monarchs that have the possessions and lives of their subjects wholly in their power to be disposed of at their mere will. "The fear of a king is as the roaring of a lion: whoso provoketh him to anger sinneth against his own soul" (Proverbs 20:2). The subject that very much enrages an arbitrary prince is liable to suffer the most extreme torments that human art can invent or human power can inflict.

But the greatest earthly potentates, in their greatest majesty and strength, and when clothed in their greatest terrors are but feeble, despicable worms of the dust in comparison to the great and almighty Creator and King of heaven and earth. It is but little that they can do when most enraged and when they have exerted the utmost of their fury. All the kings of the earth before God are as grasshoppers. They are nothing and less than nothing. Both their love and their hatred are to be despised. The wrath of the great King of kings is as much more terrible than theirs as His majesty is greater. "And I say unto you my friends, Be not afraid of them that kill the body, and after that have no more that they can do. But I will forewarn you whom you shall fear: Fear him, which after he hath killed hath power to cast into hell; yea, I say unto you, Fear him" (Luke 12:4-5).

It is the fierceness of His wrath that you are exposed to. We often read of the fury of God as in Isaiah 59:18: "According to their deeds, accordingly he will repay, fury to his adversaries." "For, behold, the Lord will come with fire, and with his chariots like a whirlwind, to render his anger with fury, and his rebuke with flames of fire" (Isaiah 66:15). And so also in many other places.

Thus we read of "the winepress of the fierceness and wrath of Almighty God" (Revelation 19:15). The words are exceedingly terrible. If only it had been said, "the wrath of God," which is infinetely dreadful. But it is said, "the fierceness and wrath of God." The fury of God! The fierceness of Jehovah! Oh, how dreadful must that be! Who can utter or conceive what such expressions carry in them! But it is not only said so, but "the fierceness and wrath of Almighty God." As though there would be a very great manifestation of His almighty power in what the fierceness of His wrath should inflict, as though omnipotence should be as it were enraged and exerted as men are wont to exert their strength in the fierceness of their wrath. Oh, then, what will be the consequence? What will become of the poor worm that shall suffer it? Whose hands can be strong? And whose heart endure? To what a dreadful, inexpressible, inconceivable depth of misery must the poor creature be sunk who shall be the subject of this?

Consider this, you who remain in an unregenerate state, that God will execute the fierceness of His anger implies that He will inflict wrath without any pity. When God beholds the ineffable extremity of your case and sees your torment so vastly disproportioned to your strength and sees how your poor soul is crushed and sinks down, as it were, into an infinite gloom, He will have no compassion upon you. He will not forbear the executions of His wrath or in the least lighten His hand. There shall be no moderation or mercy, nor will God then stay His rough wind. He will have no regard to your welfare, nor be at all careful lest you should suffer too much in any other sense, than only that you should not suffer beyond what strict justice requires. Nothing shall be withheld because it is so hard for you to bear. "Therefore will I also deal in fury; mine eye shall not spare, neither will I have pity:

and though they cry in mine ears with a loud voice, yet will I not hear them" (Ezekiel 3:18).

Now God stands ready to pity you. This is a day of mercy. You may cry now with some encouragement of obtaining mercy, but when once the day of mercy is past, your most lamentable and dolorous cries and shrieks will be in vain. You will be wholly lost and thrown away of God, as to any regard to your welfare. God will have no other use to put you to, but only to suffer misery. You shall be continued in being to no other end, for you will be a vessel of wrath fitted to destruction; and there will be no other use of this vessel, but only to be filled full of wrath. God will be so far from pitying you when you cry to Him, that it is said He will only laugh and mock (Proverbs 1:24-32).

How awful are those words of the great God! "I will tread them in mine anger, and trample them in my fury; and their blood shall be sprinkled upon my garments, and I will stain all my raiment" (Isaiah 63:3). It is perhaps impossible to conceive of words that carry in them greater manifestations of these three things—contempt, hatred, and fierceness of indignation.

If you cry to God to pity you, He will be so far from pitying you in your doleful case or showing you the least regard or favor, that instead of that He will only tread you under foot. Though He will know that you cannot bear the weight of omnipotence treading upon you, yet He will not regard that, but He will crush you under His feet without mercy. He will crush out your blood and make it fly, and it shall be sprinkled on His garments so as to stain all His raiment. He will not only hate you, but He will have you in the utmost contempt. No place shall be thought fit for you but under His feet, to be trodden down as the mire of the streets.

The misery you are exposed to is that which God will inflict to that end, that He might show what that wrath of Jehovah is. God has had it on His heart to show to angels and men, both how excellent His love is, and also how terrible His wrath is. Sometimes earthly kings show how terrible their wrath is by the extreme punishments they execute on those that provoke them. Nebuchadnezzar, that mighty and haughty monarch of the Chaldean empire, was willing to show his wrath when enraged with Shadrach, Meshach, and Abednego, and accordingly gave order that the burning fiery furnace should be heated seven times hotter than it was before. Doubtless, it was raised to the utmost degree of fierceness that human art could raise it.

But the great God is also willing to show His wrath and magnify His awful majesty and mighty power in the extreme sufferings of His enemies. "What if God, willing to show his wrath, and to make his power known, endured with much long-suffering the vessels of wrath fitted to destruction?" (Romans 9:22). And seeing this is His design and what He has determined to show how terrible the unmixed, unrestrained wrath, the fury, and fierceness of Jehovah is, He will do it to effect. There will be something accomplished and brought to pass that will be dreadful with a witness. When the great and angry God has risen up and executed His awful vengeance on the poor sinner and the wretch is actually suffering the infinite weight and power of His indignation, then will God call upon the whole universe to behold that awful majesty and mighty power that is to be seen in it. "And the people shall be as the burnings of lime: as thorns cut up shall they be burned in the fire. Hear, ye that are far off, what I have done; and ye that are near, acknowledge my might. The sinners in Zion are afraid; fearfulness hath surprised the hyprocrites. Who among us shall dwell with the devouring fire? Who among us shall dwell with everlasting burnings?" (Isaiah 33:12-14).

Thus it will be with you that are in an unconverted state, if you continue in it. The infinite might, majesty, and terribleness of the omnipotent God shall be magnified upon you in the ineffable strength of your torments. You shall be tormented in the presence of the holy angels and in the presence of the Lamb.

When you shall be in this state of suffering, the glorious inhabitants of heaven shall go forth and look on the awful spectacle, that they may see what the wrath and fierceness of the Almighty is; and when they have seen it, they will fall down and adore that great power and majesty. "And it shall come to pass, that from one new moon to another, and from one sabbath to another, shall all flesh come to worship before me, saith the Lord. And they shall go forth, and look upon the carcasses of the men that have transgressed against me: for their worm shall not die, neither shall their fire be quenched; and they shall be an abhorring unto all flesh" (Isaiah 66:23-24).

It is everlasting wrath. It would be dreadful to suffer this fierceness and wrath of almighty God one moment; but you must suffer it to all eternity. There will be no end to this exquisite, horrible misery. When you look forward you shall see a long forever, a boundless duration before you that will swallow up your thoughts and amaze your soul; and you will absolutely despair of ever having any deliverance, any end, any mitigation, any rest at all. You will know certainly that you must wear out long ages, millions of ages, in wrestling and conflicting with this almighty, merciless vengeance; and then when you have so done, when so many ages have actually been spent by you in this manner, you will know that all is but a point to what remains. So that your punishment will indeed be infinite.

Who can express what the state of a soul in such circumstances is! All that we can possibly say about it gives but a very feeble, faint representation of it. It is inexpressible and inconceivable, for "who knoweth the power of God's anger?"

How dreadful is the state of those that are daily and hourly in danger of this great wrath and infinite misery! But this is the dismal case of every soul that has not been born again, however moral and strict, sober and religious they may otherwise be. Oh, that you would consider it, whether you are young or old! There is reason to think that there are many that will actually be the subjects of this very misery to all eternity. We know not who they are or what thoughts they now have. It may be they are now at ease, hear all these things without much disturbance, and are now flattering themselves that they are not the persons, promising themselves that they shall escape. If we knew that there was one person, but one of those that we know who was to be the subject of this misery, what an awful thing it would be to think of! If we knew who it was, what an awful sight would it be to see such a person! How might every Christian lift up a lamentable and bitter cry over him! But alas, instead of one, how many is it likely will remember these solemn reflections in hell! Some may be in hell in a very short time, before this year is out. And it would be no wonder if some who are now in health, quiet and secure, should be there before tomorrow morning.

Those of you that finally continue in a natural condition, that shall keep out of hell longest, will be there in a little time! Your damnation does not slumber; it will come swiftly and, in all probability, very suddenly upon many of you. You have reason to wonder that you are not already in hell. It is doubtless the case of some that previously you have seen and known, that never deserved hell more than you, and that previously appeared as likely to have been now alive as you. Their case is past all hope; they are crying in extreme misery and perfect despair. But here you are in the land of the living and have an opportunity to obtain salvation. What would not those poor, damned, hopeless souls give for one day's opportunity such as you now enjoy!

And now you have an extraordinary opportunity, a day wherein Christ has flung the door of mercy wide open and stands in the door calling and crying with a loud voice to poor sinners; a day wherein many are flocking to Him and pressing into the kingdom of God. Many are daily coming from the east, west, north, and south; many that were very likely in the same miserable condition are now in a happy state, with their hearts filled with love to Him who has loved them and washed them from their sins in His own blood and rejoicing in hope of the glory of God.

How awful is it to be left behind at such a day! To see so many rejoicing and singing for joy of heart while you have cause to mourn for sorrow of heart and howl for vexation of spirit! How can you rest for one moment in such a condition? Are not your souls as precious as the souls of those who are flocking from day to day to Christ?

Are there not many who have lived long in the world that are not to this day born again and so are aliens from the commonwealth of Israel and have done nothing ever since they have lived but treasure up wrath against the day of wrath? Oh, your case is extremely dangerous; your guilt and hardness of heart are extremely great! Do you not see how generally persons of your years are passed over and left in the present remarkable and wonderful dispensation of God's mercy? You have need to consider yourselves and wake thoroughly out of sleep; you cannot bear the fierceness and the wrath of the infinite God.

And you who are young men and young women, will you neglect this precious season that you now enjoy, when so many others of your age are renouncing all youthful vanities and flocking to Christ? You especially have an extraordinary opportunity. But if you neglect it, it will soon be with you as it is with those persons that spent all the precious days of youth in sin and are now come to such a dreadful pass in blindness and hardness.

And you children that are unconverted, do you not know that you are going down to hell to bear the dreadful wrath of that God that is now angry with you every day and every night? Will you be content to be the children of the devil, when so many other children in the land are converted and have become the holy and happy children of the King of kings?

Let every one that is yet out of Christ and hanging over the pit of hell, whether they be old men and women or middleaged or young people or little children, now hearken to the loud calls of God's Word and providence. This acceptable year of the Lord, that is a day of such great favor to some, will doubtless be a day of as remarkable vengeance to others. Men's hearts harden and their guilt increases apace at such a day as this if they neglect their souls. And never was there so great danger of such persons being given up to hardness of heart and blindness of mind. God seems now to be hastily gathering in His elect in all parts of the land. Probably the bigger part of adult persons that ever shall be saved will be brought in now in a little time, and it will be as it was on that great outpouring of the Spirit upon the Jews in the apostles' days, the election will obtain and the rest will be blinded.

If this should be the case with you, you will eternally curse this day and will curse the day that ever you were born to see such a season of the pouring out of God's Spirit and will wish that you had died and gone to hell before you had seen it. Now, undoubtedly, it is as it was in the days of John the Baptist, the ax is in an extraordinary manner laid at "the root of the trees: therefore every tree which bringeth not forth good fruit is hewn down, and cast into the fire" (Matthew 3:10).

Therefore, let everyone that is out of Christ now awake and flee from the wrath to come. The wrath of Almighty God is now undoubtedly hanging over every unregenerate sinner. Let everyone flee out of Sodom. "Escape for thy life; look not behind thee . . . escape to the mountain, lest thou be consumed" (Genesis 19:17).

THE MOST WONDERFUL SENTENCE EVER WRITTEN

Reuben Archer Torrey

(1856-1928)

Reuben Archer Torrey was a Congregational evangelist, teacher, and author of forty books. He received his training in Yale University and Divinity School as well as at the Universities of Leipzig and Erlangen, Germany.

After he had served two pastorates, Dwight L. Moody called him to Chicago in 1889 to serve as superintendent of the new Bible Institute of the Chicago Evangelization Society (Moody Bible Institute). He also served for twelve years as the pastor of the Chicago Avenue church (now Moody Memorial Church). After Moody's death in 1899, he led the Moody Bible Institute until 1908. During that time he and Charles M. Alexander carried on successful evangelistic campaigns around the world. In Japan eighty-seven people accepted Christ as Savior in a single meeting. It is said that one world tour resulted in over 100,000 professions of faith.

From 1912 to 1924 Torrey served as dean of the Bible Institute of Los Angeles and for the last ten years also served as pastor of the Church of the Open Door. From 1924 to 1928 he devoted his time

43

to holding Bible conferences and teaching at the Moody Bible Institute.

William Culbertson, former president of Moody Bible Institute, said Torrey was a "teacher par excellence," a man of prayer, and a great personal worker.

The following sermon was delivered, with effective results, at the Church of the Open Door in Los Angeles. It was taken down in shorthand and edited by Dr. Torrey.

THE MOST WONDERFUL SENTENCE EVER WRITTEN

"For God so loved the world, that He gave His only begotten Son, that whosoever believeth in Him should not perish, but have everlasting life"
(John 3:16).

MY TEXT IS "The Most Wonderful Sentence That Was Ever Written." Of course that sentence is in the Bible. All the greatest sentences that were ever written are found in one book, God's Word, the Bible. The Bible is a book that abounds in illuminating, stirring, startling, marvelous, bewildering, amazing, and life-transforming utterances; utterances with which there is absolutely nothing to compare in all the other literature of the world. But I am inclined to think that the one we are to consider tonight is the most remarkable of them all. I think that after we have given it careful thought you will agree with me that this sentence is the most wonderful that was ever written.

The Most Wonderful Sentence Ever Written

You are all perfectly familiar with it. I doubt if there is a person in this audience who has not heard it again and again. Indeed our very familiarity with it has blinded many of us to the wonderful character of it and the stupendous significance of it. But we are going to look at it steadily and closely, turning it around and around—as one would turn around and scrutinize a diamond of unusual purity, beauty, brilliance, and play of prismatic colors—until its beauty, its profundity, its glory, its sublimity, and its amazing significance are more fully seen and appreciated by us.

The sentence is found in John 3:16, "For God so loved the world, that he gave his only begotten Son, that whosoever believeth in him should not perish, but have everlasting life." There are whole volumes of incomparably precious truth packed into that one sentence. Indeed many volumes have been devoted to the exposition of that one verse, but it is not exhausted yet and never will be. These marvelous words of God never become hackneyed or worn out or wearisome. We are always beholding new beauty and new glory in them. When all the millions of volumes that men have written in many languages throughout the many centuries of literary history have become obsolete and are forgotten, that imperishable sentence shall shine out in its matchless beauty and peerless glory throughout the endless ages of eternity.

Let me repeat it again. "For God so loved the world, that he gave his only begotten Son, that whosoever believeth in him should not perish, but have everlasting life." God Himself has used that statement to save thousands of souls, to lift men out of the sad—yes, appalling—ruin that sin had wrought into the glory of likeness to Himself. I trust that He may use it tonight to save many more.

The verse tells us five exceedingly important facts. First, God's attitude toward the world; second, God's attitude toward sin; third, God's attitude toward His Son; fourth, God's attitude toward all who beleive in His Son; fifth, God's attitude toward all who refuse or neglect to believe in His Son.

First of all, *this verse from God's Word tells us what God's attitude is toward the world*. What is God's attitude toward the world? *LOVE*. The sentence reads, "God so *LOVED* the world." Love is the most wonderful thing in the world, and love is one of the most uncommon things in the world.

There is in the world today much that is called "love," but most of that which is called love is not love at all. We speak oftentimes of a young man's "love" for a young woman, and all we mean by it is that this young man wishes to get that young woman for his own pleasure and gratification. That is not love at all; it oftentimes has not the slightest semblance of love. It is oftentimes utter selfishness and not infrequently the vilest and most unbridled lust.

It is not at all unlikely that if the young woman refuses to accept him as a husband or so-called "lover," he will shoot her down or seek to blast her reputation. And that hideous thing we call "love!" He *"loved"* her so much that he killed her. It is really as remote from love as anything possibly can be, as remote from love as hell is from heaven. It is the very lowest order of selfishness and the grossest beastliness.

When a lawyer in this city week before last shot

his former wife because she would not return to him and endure longer the outrages that he had inflicted upon her for years, was it love that prompted his amazingly cowardly, sneaking, cruel, ruffianly, devilish act? No, it was a passion that would have disgraced the lowest wild beast of the jungle.

We speak of one man's love for another. What do we usually mean? Only this—the two men are friendly because in many respects they are congenial and enjoy one another's society. But if one does some little thing that offends the other, the so-called love is turned into utter indifference or even into bitter hate. It was never "love." It was mere self-centered fondness.

All this is not love. What is love? *Love is the consuming, absorbing desire for and delight in another's highest good.* Real love is entirely unselfish. It loses sight utterly of self-interest and sets itself to seeking the interest of the person loved. This was God's attitude toward the world. He *loved* the world, really loved it.

He looked down upon this world, the whole mass of men living at any time upon it and that should live upon it in all times to come, and He loved them all. His whole being went out in infinite yearning to benefit and bless the world. Any cost to Himself would be disregarded if it would bless the world to pay the cost. "God so loved the world that *he gave his only begotten Son.*" Oh, men and women, stand and wonder! Oh, angels and archangel, cherubim and seraphim, stand and wonder! "God *so* loved the world *that he gave his only begotten Son.*"

Some men tell us that they cannot believe the Bible to be the Word of God because there are so many incredible statements in it. But that is the most incredible statement in the whole Book, and yet we know it is true. If I can believe that statement I ought not to have any difficulty with any other statement in the whole Book, and I can believe that statement. I do believe that statement. I know that statement is true. I have put it to the test of personal experience and found it true. "God so loved the world that He gave His only begotten Son"; that has been God's attitude toward the world from the beginning. That is God's attitude toward the world tonight.

God loves the *world*. There are men and women and children in this world whom you and I love, but God loves the whole world. There is not a man in it, not a woman in it, not a child in it whom God does not love. From the intellectually most rarely gifted and morally most saintly man and woman down to the most apelike and ignorant and the morally most degraded and brutelike man or woman, God loves each and every one. "God so loved the *world*."

There are hundreds and hundreds of people who gather in this church about whom you care absolutely nothing. You never saw them before; you will never see them again. If you should read in your paper tomorrow morning, "John Jones, who was at the Church of the Open Door, as he was going home from the meeting, got in front of a Sixth Street car and was instantly killed," you would hardly give it a second thought. John Jones is nothing to you.

But John Jones is something to God. God loves John Jones, and John Smith, and John Johnson, and every other man and woman and child. You may be a very lonely stranger in a great city's crowd. Perhaps you have been unfortunate and are penniless and friendless; perhaps you have gone down into some black depth of sin, and you say to yourself, "Not one person in this great crowd has the slightest interest in me." That may be true. But there is One who has an interest in you. There is One who so loved you that He "gave his only begotten Son" to die for you, and that One is God. God loves the world and every one in it. God loves the world in the purest, deepest, and highest sense of that word *love*. Yes, God loves you. "Whom do you mean by *you*?" someone asks. I mean every man, woman, and child.

There is nothing about the world that God should love it. It is a sinful world, it is a selfish world, it is a corrupt world. The more I get to know the world of which I am a part, and the more I get to know myself, the more I am humbled. John was entirely right when he said, "The whole world lieth in wickedness" (1 John 5:19).

I am an optimist, but I am not an optimist by painting a black world white. Look at the rich world. What a cruel thing it is. How it marches on, trampling down every one that lies in its path to obtain greater wealth. How are great fortunes usually built up? You know. I know—by the trampling of human hearts underfoot.

But look at the poor world. It is nearly as cruel as the rich world. One day in Chicago two men were working hard to make an honest living for themselves and their families, just four doors north of the church of which I was pastor. Four other poor men sneaked in, chopped their heads open with hatchets, and ran. Why did they do it? Simply because they wanted the jobs of those two men. The two men struck down by the four heartless cowards were guilty of no crime and no wrong against the ones that cut them down. They did not belong to the union, that was all.

If you wish to know the spirit of the rich world, look at some of the greedy, conscienceless trusts. If you wish to know the spirit of the poor world, look at the present day methods of the trades unions. The spirit of both is essentially the same—greed for gold; money must be secured at any cost, even the cost of murder of others by the slow process of starvation on the part of the rich or the rapid process of hatchet and bullet and dynamite on the part of the poor.

A cruel, selfish, bloodthirsty world is this. What the world really is we saw in the late war [1914-1918.—Ed.]. But God loves it. God loves those four cowards who cut down their fellow laboring men. God loves those millionaires who, already having more than is for their own good or for the good of their families, are trying to increase their wealth by crowding competitors to the wall and their families to the poorhouse. God loves those moral monsters that made Europe flow with blood and gasp with poison gas. God loves the world.

As I come to know more and more of the cruelty, the greed, the selfishness, the falsehood, the villainy, the lust, the vileness, and the beastliness there is in this world—in the social world, high and low, in the business world in all its departments, and in the political world—I sometimes almost wonder why God does not blot out this whole world as He did Sodom and Gomorrah of old. Why does He not do it? I will tell you why. God *loves* the world. In spite of all its cruelty, in spite of all its greed, in spite of all its selfishness, in spite of all its lust, in spite of all its vileness in thought, word, and deed, God loves the world. Is it not wonderful, is it not amazing that a holy God should love a sinful world like this? But He does.

There is not a man whom God does not love. There is not a woman whom God does not love. There is not a thief whom God does not love. There is not a woman who has forgotten her modesty and her true womanhood that God does not love. There is not an adulterer whom God does not love, not a sinner, not an outcast, not a criminal of any kind whom God does not love. "God so loved the *world*."

Years ago I said to a woman, in deep despair because of the depths of iniquity and infamy into which she had fallen, "God loves you."

"Not me, Mr. Torrey. God doesn't love me. I have killed a man," she cried.

"Yes, I know that, but God loves you."

"No, not me. I have murdered innocent, unborn babes."

"Yes, I know that, but God loves you."

"Not me. My heart is as hard as a rock."

"Yes, but God loves you."

"Not me. I have prayed to the devil to take away all my convictions, and he has done it."

"Yes, I know all that, but God loves you."

Then I made that woman get down on her knees, and she came to believe in God's love to her and found a great peace. I saw her again last month when I was in Chicago. She came down to the platform to speak to me at the close of one of my meetings.

She said, "Do you know me?"

I replied, "Of course, I know you," and called her by name.

Her face was wreathed with smiles. "Oh," she said, "Mr. Torrey, I am still at the old work of winning others to Christ."

Ah, some of you self-righteous skeptics hold up your hands in holy horror and disgust and say, "I don't want to believe in a God who welcomes sinners so vile as that." You miserable pharisee, you old hypocrite, you are essentially as bad as she once was and infinitely worse than she now is. But God loves you, even you. God's attitude toward the whole wide world is love.

But what is God's attitude toward sin? Our text tells us, *God's attitude toward sin is HATE*. God loves the world with infinite love. God hates sin with infinite hate. How does our text show that? Listen. "God *so* loved the world, *that he gave his only begotten Son*, that whosoever believeth in him should not perish, but have everlasting life." How does that show that God hates sin? In this way: if God had not hated sin He could have saved the world He loved without an atonement, without the atonement that cost Him so much, the death and agony of His only begotten Son, who died as an atoning sacrifice on the cross.

Because God was holy and therefore hated sin, hated it with infinite hatred, His hatred of sin must manifest itself somehow, either in the punishment of the sinner—and the banishment of the sinner forever from Himself from life, and from hope—or in some other way. But God's love would not permit the just punishment of the sinner. So God in the person of His Son took the penalty of sin upon Himself and thus saved the world He loved. "All we like sheep have gone astray; we have turned every one to his own way; and Jehovah *hath made to strike on him* the iniquity of us all" (Isaiah 53:6, literal translation; italics added). In this way God made possible the salvation that He Himself purchased for men by the atoning death of His only begotten Son.

The cross of Christ declares two things: first, God's infinite love of the world; second, God's infinite hatred of sin. Oh, wicked man, do not fancy that because God loves you He will wink at your sin. Not for one moment. He hates your sin, He hates your greed, He hates your selfishness, He hates your lying, He hates your drunkenness, He hates your impure imagination, He hates your moral uncleanness, He hates your beastliness, He hates every sin, great and small, of which you are guilty. The hatred of a true man for all falsehood, the hatred of honest men for all dishonesty, the hatred of a true, pure woman for the unspeakable vileness of the woman of the street and gutter is nothing to the blazing wrath of God at your smallest sin. Nevertheless, God loves you.

This wonderful verse also tells of God's attitude toward His Son. What is God's attitude toward His Son? Listen. "God so loved the world that he gave *his only begotten son.*" *God's attitude toward His Son, "his only begotten Son," is infinite love.* The Lord Jesus is the only Son of God. We become sons of God through our faith in Him, but He is the only Son of God by eternal and inherent right. He was the object of His Father's infinite love in the measureless ages before any one of the worlds was created—yes, before there was angel or archangel or any of the heavenly beings.

Let me speak to you, fathers. What is your attitude toward your son? How you love him! And if you have only one son, how intensely you love him. I have but one son. I have longed for more, but God in His wisdom has seen fit to give us but one son. How I love him! God only knows how I love him. But my love to my one son is nothing, nothing at all compared to God's love for His only begotten Son.

I sometimes think of my boy and fancy I know something of God's love for Jesus Christ, but it is only a little, a very little that I know. But though God thus loved His Son, God gave that Son whom He so infinitely loved, that Son who through all eternity had been the object of His delight, God gave that only begotten Son for the world, for you and for me. He gave Him to leave heaven and His own companionship to come down to earth to live a lonely stranger here. He gave Him to be spit upon and buffeted and "despised and rejected of men." He gave Him to be crowned with thorns, mocked at, and derided. He gave Him to be dragged through the streets before a howling, yelling, jeering mob. He gave Him to be nailed to the cross—yes, to a cross—and to hang there in misery, pain, and agony for hours, the object of the rude jests and jeers of the merciless mob. He gave Him to die of a "broken heart," a heart broken by the reproach of the men He loved (Psalm 69:20) and by grief over man's sins, which He had taken upon Himself. Yes, God gave Him *His only begotten Son*, thus to be separated from Himself, to suffer, and to die. Why? Because God loved you and me, and that was the only price that would purchase our salvation. And God paid that price, that awful price.

The Most Wonderful Sentence Ever Written

Oh, it is wonderful! I can think of but one other thing that is anywhere near as wonderful as the love of God for sinners. What is that? The way we treat that love. The way men treat it. The way some of you despise it. The way you reject it. The way you trample it underfoot. The way you even try to doubt it, disbelieve it, deny it, discredit it, and try to make yourself think that you have "intellectual difficulties about the doctrine of the atonement."

People, at least be honest. Your real difficulty is not intellectual—you want to save your pride and excuse the enormity of your ingratitude. To do that you do not hesitate at the gross sin of even denying the Lord that bought you, bought you by His atoning agony and death (2 Peter 2:1). Oh, be honest with the wondrous love of God, even if you are determined to spurn it. Your pretended "theological difficulties with the atonement" that Jesus Christ made upon the cross are simply your dishonest attempt to excuse your abominable ingratitude and damnable rejection of infinite love. Bear with me for talking thus plainly about your sin. I do it in love to you. You may not be willing to admit that tonight, but you will have to admit it in that day when you stand in the light of the great white throne where all lies and pretexts and deceptions and hypocrisies will be burned up.

Now let us look at another thing: *what the sentence teaches about God's attitude toward believers in the Lord Jesus Christ.* What is God's attitude toward all who believe in Jesus Christ? It can be put in a few words. *God's attitude toward all believers in Jesus Christ is to give them eternal life.* "God so loved the world, that he gave his only begotten Son, *that whosoever believeth in him should*

not perish, but have everlasting life." The death of
Jesus Christ has opened for all who believe in Him
a way of pardon and made it possible for a holy
God to forgive sin and to give eternal life to the
vilest sinner if only he will believe in Jesus Christ.
"The wages of sin is death" (Romans 6:23), and
these wages must be paid; but Jesus Christ paid the
price, so life and not death is possible for you and
me—"the gift of God is eternal life through Christ
Jesus our Lord" (Romans 6:23). *Whosoever* believes
on Jesus Christ, whom God gave to die for him, can
have eternal life, yes, does have eternal life. Anyone
can have eternal life. There is but one condition—
just believe on Jesus Christ. You ought to do it any-
how, even if there were nothing to be gained by
your believing in Him; you owe it to Jesus Christ to
believe on Him. He is infinitely worthy of your
faith.

But there *is* something to be gained by believing
on Him, something of infinite worth—eternal life.
Do you wish eternal life? You can have it. Anyone
can have it, no matter what his past may have been.
"God so loved the world, that he gave his only begotten Son, that *whosoever believeth* in him should
not perish, but have everlasting life." Oh, if I offered
you great honor it would be nothing compared with
this. If I offered you enormous wealth it would be
nothing compared with this. If I offered you exempt-
ion from all sickness and pain it would be nothing
compared with this. *Eternal life!* That is what God
offers. And God offers it to each one of you. Oh,
how it makes the heart swell and throb with hope
and joy and rapture—eternal life!

There is just one thing left to mention, and that is
God's attitude toward all those who will not believe

on Jesus Christ. What is it? Listen. "For God so loved the world, that he gave his only begotten Son, that *whosoever believeth in him should not perish,* but have everlasting life." *God's attitude toward those who will not believe in Jesus Christ, those who prefer sin and vanity and pride to the glorious Son of God, is simply this: God with great grief and reluctance withdraws from them the infinite gift He has purchased at so great cost and which they will not accept. God leaves them to perish.* There is no hope for any man who rejects God's gift of eternal life, obtained by simply believing in His only begotten Son. God has exhausted all the possibilities of a saving love and power in Jesus Christ's atonement on the cross of Calvary. Reject Him, neglect to accept Him, and you must eternally perish.

God's attitude toward the world is infinite love; God's attitude toward sin is infinite hatred. God's attitude toward His Son is unutterable love, but He gave up that Son to die for you and me. God's attitude toward the believer is to give him eternal life, regardless of what his past has been. God's attitude toward those who will not believe is to leave them to the perdition they so madly choose. Men and women, what will you choose tonight, life or death? Some of you will decide that question in a few minutes, decide it for all eternity. May God help you to decide it right.

One night in Minneapolis years ago, I knelt in prayer beside a young woman who was having an awful struggle. A fearful battle was going on in her soul between the forces of light and the forces of darkness. She heard God calling her to accept His love and to accept the eternal life that that love had purchased by the atoning death of His own Son. But she heard other voices too, voices of the world, and the voice of Satan himself, luring her to turn her back upon Jesus Christ and choose the world. It was awful to watch the battle, my heart ached as I watched the battle, and I kept crying to God that the Holy Spirit might gain the victory. Now and then I spoke to her. Finally I took out my watch and said, "This battle cannot last much longer. Continue to resist the Holy Spirit as you are resisting Him now, and you will seal your doom. I believe if you do not yield to God in the next ten minutes that you will never yield but will be lost forever." Then I prayed but said nothing more to her, but now and again looked at my watch. The fight went on. Which way would she decide! Before the ten minutes were up she yielded to God.

There is a like battle going on in the hearts of some who are reading these words. Some of you have been brought to realize the wondrous love of God for you as you have never realized it before. Some of you have been brought to see that eternal life is possible for you today if you will only choose Christ. But the power of the world and of sin and of Satan is strong upon you still, and the world, sin, and above all Satan will not let you go without making a mighty effort to keep you in his power, to blind you, and to forever destroy your soul.

Oh, men and women out of Christ, each and every one of you, look, look, look! Look once more at the cross of Christ. See Him hanging there in awful agony, paying the penalty of your sin, and as you look, listen once more to the precious words of the most wonderful sentence that was ever written, "God so loved the world, that he gave his only begotten Son, that whosoever believeth in him should not perish, but have everlasting life." What will you do with that love tonight? Will you yield to it and believe on the Savior and obtain eternal life? Or will you trample that wondrous love of God underfoot, and say again tonight as you have often said before, "I will not accept Christ," and go out to perish, perish eternally?

One night many years ago, I was preaching the first sermon I ever preached in the city of Chicago. (It was some years before I went there to live.) I was at the first International Convention of Christian Workers. The morning the convention opened I entered a little late, and the nominating committee was just bringing in its report. To my amazement, I heard them announce my name as nominated for chairman of the convention and president of the International Christian Workers' Association. I was not yet thirty years old, and there were many workers there who knew far more about aggressive methods of Christian work than I had ever learned.

However, there was nothing to do but to accept the position, and during the days of that wonderful convention I occupied the chairman's seat. The convention was held in the old First Methodist Church in the heart of the city, at the corner of Washington and Clark streets.

When Sunday came, of course the church held its own services, but I was invited to preach at the evening service. There had been much prayer, and the Spirit of God was present in great power; when I gave the invitation many rose to say that they would accept Jesus Christ as their Savior and then came down to the altar. Among those who had risen I noticed a beautifully dressed lady near the front, an intelligent looking woman, but I noticed also that she did not come to the altar with the others. While the altar service was in progress I stepped down and urged her to come to the front, but she refused.

On Monday night at the regular session of the convention I saw her come in and take a seat just a few rows from the back of the building. When the meeting was drawing to a close I called Mayor Howland of Toronto (who was vice-president of the convention) to the chair and slipped down to the back of the church in order that I might speak with that lady before she got out of the building. The moment the benediction was pronounced I hastened to her side and asked if she would remain a few moments. As the others filed out she sat down, and I took a seat beside her and commenced to urge upon her an immediate and whole-hearted acceptance of Jesus Christ.

"Let me tell you my story," she replied. "I have attended a Sunday school in this city ever since I was a little girl. I scarcely missed a Sunday." (She told me what Sunday school it was—one of the aristocratic Sunday schools on the North Side.) "But," she continued, "though I have been going to Sunday school all these years, do you know that you are the first person in all my life that ever spoke to me personally about my accepting Christ?"

Then she went on to tell me the story of her life. She was unusually well-educated, occupying a high position of responsibility, but the story that she told me of her career was so shameless that I was amazed that a woman of sense, to say nothing of character, would dream of telling such a story to a man. Then she hurried on and told me how she had passed the preceding Easter Sunday. It was a story

The Most Wonderful Sentence Ever Written

I could not repeat. Having finished, she said with a mocking laugh, "Funny way to spend Easter, wasn't it?"

I was astounded and shocked. I did not attempt to say anything in reply; I did not wish to. I simply opened my Bible to John 3:16, handed it to her, and asked her to read. It was a diamond print Bible, and she had to hold it close to her face to see the words. She began to read with a smile on her lips, "For God so loved the world"—the smile vanished as she read on—"that he gave his only begotten Son." She choked and broke down; the tears literally poured from her eyes on the page of the Bible and on the beautiful silk dress she wore. The love of God had conquered that sinful, hardened, trifling, seemingly shameless heart.

Oh, friend, I would that that love might break your heart, break down your hardness, unbelief, worldliness, and resistance to God and His love. See the Lord Jesus hanging on yonder cross in unutterable agony, in indescribable pain, His heart breaking for you, breaking for your sins, and hear again this most wonderful sentence that was ever written, "For God so loved the world, that he gave his only begotten Son, that whosoever believeth in him should not perish, but have everlasting life."

GOD'S LOVE TO FALLEN MAN

John Wesley

(1703-1791)

It is said that John Wesley preached 40,000 sermons and traveled 250,000 miles, mostly by horseback.

Wesley was not satisfied to preach a sermon without some definite follow-up program. Everywhere he went, he tried to establish a local "preaching house." This led to the societies that became the nuclei of the Methodist church.

When he packed the "preaching houses," he would take to the open air, seeking to reach all classes of people. He sometimes preached on hell, but preferred to speak on the love of God, a theme that prevails in his sermons. These sermons were simple, straight, direct appeals spoken from the heart to the heart. He did not waste superfluous words. The sermons were sometimes written out but usually well outlined.

John Wesley and George Whitefield were contemporary preachers. But about 1740 a breach between the two men developed because of doctrinal differences. Wesley published a sermon on "Free Grace" in which he adopted into his creed the doctrine of sinless perfection. This Whitefield could not embrace. He vigorously preached the doctine of election.

While the two could never agree on these two doctrines, they still had genuine love one for the other in Christ. On one occasion Whitefield was asked who should preach his funeral sermon. Without hesitation he replied, "John Wesley." When Whitefield died in America in 1770, Wesley preached the funeral sermon in the chapel on Tottenham Court Road and again in the Tabernacle at Greenwich—on both occasions to overflow congregations.

GOD'S LOVE TO FALLEN MAN

Not as the offense, so also is the free gift (Romans 5:15).

How EXCEEDINGLY COMMON, and how bitter, is the outcry against our first parent for the mischief that he not only brought upon himself but entailed upon his latest posterity! It was by his willful rebellion against God "that sin entered into the world." "By one man's disobedience," as the apostle observes, "the many," as many as were then in the loins of their forefather, "were made," or constituted, "sinners": not only deprived of the favor of God, but also of His image, of all virtue, righteousness, and true holiness; and sunk, partly into the image of the devil—in pride, malice, and all other diabolical tempers—brutal passions and groveling appetites. Hence also death entered into the world, with all his forerunners and attendants; pain, sickness, and a whole train of uneasy, as well as unholy, passions and tempers.

"For all this we may thank Adam," has been echoed down from generation to generation. The same charge has been repeated in every age and every nation where the oracles of God are known; in which alone this grand and important event has been discovered to the children of men. Has not your heart and probably your lips too joined in the general charge? How few are there of those who believe the scriptural relation of the fall of man that have not entertained the same thought concerning our first parent, severely condemning him that, through willful disobedience to the sole command of his Creator,

Brought death into the world, and all our woe.

Nay, it were well if the charge rested here, but it is certain it does not. It cannot be denied that it frequently glances from Adam to his Creator. Have not thousands, even of those that are called Christians, taken the liberty to call His mercy, if not His justice also, into question on this very account? Some indeed have done this a little more modestly, in an oblique and indirect manner. But others have thrown aside the mask and asked, "Did not God foresee that Adam would abuse his liberty? And did He not know the baneful consequences that it must naturally have on all His posterity? And why then did He permit that disobedience? Was it not easy for the Almighty to have prevented it?"

God certainly did foresee the whole. This cannot be denied. For "known unto God are all his works from the beginning of the world": rather from all eternity. And it was undoubtedly in His power to prevent it; for He has all power both in heaven and earth. But it was known to Him at the same time that it was best upon the whole not to prevent it. He knew that "not as the transgression, so is the free gift"; that the evil resulting from the former was not as the good resulting from the latter, not worthy to be compared with it. He saw that to permit the fall of the first man was far best for mankind in general; that abundantly more good than evil would accrue to the posterity of Adam by his fall; that if "sin abounded" thereby over all the earth, yet grace "would much more abound"; yea, and that to every individual of the human race unless it was his own choice.

It is exceedingly strange that hardly anything has been written, or at least published, on this subject. Nay, that it has been so little weighed or understood by the generality of Christians; especially considering that it is not a matter of mere curiosity, but a truth of the deepest importance; it being impossible, on any other principle,

> *To assert a gracious providence,*
> *And justify the ways of God with men,*

and considering withal how plain this important truth is to all sensible and candid inquirers. May the Lover of men open the eyes of our understanding to perceive clearly that by the fall of Adam mankind in general has gained a capacity

First, of being more holy and happy on earth; and,

Second, of being more happy in heaven than otherwise they could have been.

Mankind in general has gained by the fall of

Adam a capacity of attaining more holiness and happiness on earth than it would have been possible for them to attain if Adam had not fallen. For if Adam had not fallen, Christ had not died. Nothing can be clearer than this, nothing more undeniable. The more thoroughly we consider the point, the more deeply shall we be convinced of it. Unless all the partakers of human nature had received that deadly wound in Adam, it would not have been needful for the Son of God to take our nature upon Him. This was the very ground of His coming into the world. "By one man sin entered into the world, and death by sin; and so death passed upon all men," through Him in whom all men sinned (Romans 5:12). Was it not to remedy this very thing that "the Word was made flesh," that as in Adam all died, even so in Christ all might be made alive?

Unless then many had been made sinners by the disobedience of one; by the obedience of one, many would not have been made righteous (v. 19), so there would have been no room for that amazing display of the Son of God's love to mankind. There would have been no occasion for His being "obedient unto death, even the death of the cross."

It could not then have been said, to the astonishment of all the hosts of heaven, "God so loved the world," yea, the ungodly world that had no thought or desire of returning to Him, "that he gave his Son" out of His bosom, His only begotten Son, "to the end that whosoever believeth on him should not perish, but have everlasting life." Neither could we then have said, "God was in Christ reconciling the world to himself"; or that he "made him to be sin," that is, a sin offering "for us, who knew no sin; that we might be made the righteousness of God in him." There would have been no occasion for such "an advocate with the Father,"as "Jesus Christ the righteous"; neither for His appearing "at the right hand of God, to make intercession for us."

What is the necessary consequence of this? It is this: There could then have been no such thing as faith in God thus loving the world, giving His only Son for us men and for our salvation. There could have been no such thing as faith in the Son of God, as "loving us and giving himself for us." There could have been no faith in the Spirit of God, as renewing the image of God in our hearts, as raising us from the death of sin to the life of righteousness. Indeed the whole privilege of justification by faith could have no existence; there could have been no redemption in the blood of Christ; neither could Christ have been "made of God unto us," either "wisdon, righteousness, sanctification," or "redemption."

And the same grand blank that was in our faith must likewise have been in our love. We might have loved the Author of our being, the Father of angels and men, as our Creator and Preserver. We might have said, "O Lord our Governor, how excellent is Thy name in all the earth?" but we could not have loved Him under the nearest and dearest relation, "as delivering up his Son for us all." We might have loved the Son of God as being "the brightness of his Father's glory, the express image of his person"; (although this ground seems to belong rather to the inhabitants of heaven than earth); but we could not have loved Him as "bearing our sins in his own body on the tree," and "by that one oblation of himself once offered, making a full sacrifice, oblation, and satisfaction for the sins of the whole world."

We could not have been "made conformable to his death," nor have known "the power of his resurrection." We could not have loved the Holy Spirit, as revealing to us the Father and the Son; as opening the eyes of our understanding; bringing us out of darkness into His marvelous light; renewing the image of God in our soul and sealing us to the day of redemption.

So that, in truth, what is now "in the sight of God even the Father," not of fallible men, "pure religion and undefiled," would then have had no being; inasmuch as it wholly depends on those grand principles: "By grace ye are saved through faith"; and "Jesus Christ is of God made unto us wisdom, and righteousness, and sanctification, and redemption."

We see then what unspeakable advantage we derive from the fall of our first parent with regard to faith; faith both in God the Father, who spared not His own Son, His only Son, but "wounded him for our transgressions," and bruised Him "for our iniquities"; and in God the Son who poured out His soul for us transgressors and washed us in His own blood. We see what advantage we derive with regard to the love of God; both of God the Father and God the Son. The chief ground of this love, as long as we remain in the body, is plainly declared by the apostle: "We love him, because he first loved us." But the greatest instance of His love would have never been given, if Adam had not fallen.

And as our faith, both in God the Father and the Son, receives an unspeakable increase, if not its very being, from this grand event, as does also our love both of the Father and the Son; so does the love of our neighbor also, our benevolence to all mankind, which cannot but increase in the same

69

proportion with our faith and love of God. For who does not apprehend the force of that inference drawn by the loving apostle? "Beloved, if God so loved us, we ought also to love one another." If God so loved us! Observe, the stress of the argument lies on this very point; so loved us as to deliver up His only Son to die a cursed death for our salvation. Beloved, what manner of love is this, wherewith God hath loved us; so as to give His only Son, in glory equal with the Father, in majesty co-eternal?

What manner of love is this wherewith the only begotten Son of God hath loved us, as to empty Himself, as far as possible, of His eternal Godhead; to divest Himself of that glory that He had with the Father before the world began; to take upon Him the form of a servant, being found in fashion as a man; and then to humble Himself still further, "being obedient unto death, even the death of the cross!" If God so loved us, how ought we to love one another? But this motive to brotherly love had been totally wanting if Adam had not fallen. Consequently we could not then have loved one another in so high a degree as we may now. Nor could there have been that height and depth in the command of our blessed Lord, "As I have loved you, so love one another."

Such gainers we may be by Adam's fall, with regard both to the love of God and of our neighbor. But there is another grand point that though little adverted to, deserves our deepest consideration. By that one act of our first parent, not only "sin entered into the world" but pain also, and was alike entailed on his whole posterity. And herein appeared, not only the justice, but the unspeakable goodness of God. For how much good does He continually bring out of this evil! How much holiness and happiness out of pain!

How innumerable are the benefits that God conveys to the children of men through the channel of sufferings! So that it might well be said, "What are termed afflictions in the language of men, are in the language of God styled blessings." Indeed, had there been no suffering in the world, a considerable part of religion, yes, and in some respects, the most excellent part, could have had no place therein; since the very existence of it depends on our suffering; so that had there been no pain, it could have had no being.

Upon this foundation, even our suffering, it is evident all our passive graces are built; yea, the noblest of all Christian graces, "Love enduring all things." Here is the ground for resignation to God, enabling us to say from the heart, in every trying hour, "It is the Lord: let him do what seemeth him good." "Shall we receive good at the hand of the Lord, and shall we not receive evil?"

And what a glorious spectacle is this! Did it not constrain even a heathen to cry out, "*Ecce spectaculum Deo dignum!*" See a sight worthy of God; a good man struggling with adversity and superior to it. Here is the ground for confidence in God, both with regard to what we feel and with regard to what we should fear, were it not that our soul is calmly stayed on Him. What room could there be for trust in God, if there were no such thing as pain or danger? Who might not say then, "The cup which my Father hath given me, shall I not drink it?" It is by sufferings that our faith is tried, and therefore made more acceptable to God. It is in the day of trouble that we have occasion to say,

John Wesley

"Though he slay me, yet will I trust in him." And this is well-pleasing to God, that we should own Him in the face of danger; in defiance of sorrow, sickness, pain, or death.

Had there been neither natural nor moral evil in the world, what must have become of patience, meekness, gentleness, longsuffering? It is manifest they could have had no being; seeing all these have evil for their object. If, therefore, evil had never entered into the world, neither could these have had any place in it. For who could have returned good for evil, had there been no evil doer in the universe? How had it been possible, on that supposition to "overcome evil with good"? Will you say, "But all these graces might have been divinely infused into the hearts of men"? Undoubtedly they might: but if they had, there would have been no use or exercise for them. Whereas in the present state of things we can never long want occasion to exercise them; and the more they are exercised, the more all our graces are strengthened and increased.

And in the same proportion as our resignation our confidence in God, our patience and fortitude, our meekness, gentleness, and longsuffering, together with our faith and love of God and man increase, must our happiness increase, even in the present world.

As God's permission of Adam's fall gave all his posterity a thousand opportunities of suffering and thereby of exercising all those passive graces that increase both their holiness and happiness; so it gives them opportunities of doing good in numberless instances; of exercising themselves in various good works that otherwise could have had no being. And what exertions of benevolence, of compassion,

of Godlike mercy, had then been totally prevented?
Who could then have said to the lover of men,

Thy mind throughout my life be shown;
  While listening to the wretch's cry,
The widow's or the orphan's groan,
  On mercy's wings I swiftly fly,
The poor and needy to relieve;
  Myself, my all for them to give?

It is the just observation of a benevolent man,

  All worldly joys are less,
Than that one joy of doing kindnesses.

Surely in keeping this commandment, if no other, there is great reward. "As we have time, let us do good unto all men"; good of every kind and in every degree. Accordingly the more good we do (other circumstances being equal), the happier we shall be. The more we deal our bread to the hungry, cover the naked with garments, the more we relieve the stranger, visit them that are sick or in prison, the more kind offices we do to those that groan under the various evils of human life, the more comfort we receive even in the present world, the greater the recompense we have in our own bosom.

To sum up what has been said under this head: the more holy we are upon earth, the more happy we must be (seeing there is an inseparable connection between holiness and happiness); as the more good we do to others, the more of present reward redounds into our own bosom; even as our sufferings for God lead us to rejoice in Him "with joy unspeakable and full of glory." Therefore, the fall of Adam—first, by giving us an opportunity of being far more holy; second, by giving us the occasions of doing innumerable good works that otherwise could not have been done, and third, by putting it into our power to suffer for God, whereby "the Spirit of glory and of God resteth upon us"—may be of such advantage to the children of men, even in the present life that they will not thoroughly comprehend till they attain life everlasting.

It is then we shall be enabled fully to comprehend not only the advantages that accrue at the present time to the sons of men by the fall of their first parent, but the infinitely greater advantages that they may reap from it in eternity.

In order to form some conception of this we may remember the observation of the apostle. As "one star differeth from another star in glory, so also is the resurrection of the dead." The most glorious stars will undoubtedly be those who are the most holy, who bear most of that image of God wherein they were created; the next in glory will be those who have been most abundant in good works; and next to them, those that have suffered most according to the will of God.

But what advantages, in every one of these respects, will the children of God receive in heaven by God's permitting the introduction of pain upon earth in consequence of sin? By occasion of this they attained many holy tempers that otherwise could have had no being—resignation to God; confidence in Him, in times of trouble and danger; patience, meekness, gentleness, longsuffering, and the whole train of passive virtues: and on account of this superior holiness, they will then enjoy superior happiness.

Again, every one will then "receive his own reward, according to his own labor": every individual will be "rewarded according to his work." But the Fall gave rise to innumerable good works, which could otherwise never have existed; such as ministering to the necessities of saints; yea, relieving the distressed in every kind: and hereby innumerable stars will be added to their eternal crown.

Yet again, there will be an abundant reward in heaven for suffering, as well as for doing the will of God. "These light afflictions, which are but for a moment, work out for us a far more exceeding and eternal weight of glory." Therefore that event, which occasioned the entrance of suffering into the world, has thereby occasioned to all the children of God an increase of glory to all eternity. For although the sufferings themselves will be at an end; although

The pain of life shall then be o'er,
The anguish and distracting care;
There sighing grief shall weep no more:
And sin shall never enter there;

the joys occasioned thereby shall never end, but flow at God's right hand forevermore.

There is one advantage more that we reap from Adam's fall that is not unworthy our attention. Unless in Adam all had died, being in the loins of their first parent, every descendant of Adam, every child of man, must have personally answered for himself to God. It seems to be a necessary consequence of this, that if he had once fallen, once violated any command of God, there would have been no possibility of his rising again; there was no help, but he must have perished without remedy. For that covenant knew not to show mercy. The word was, "The soul that sinneth, it shall die."

Who would not rather be on the footing he is on

now under a covenant of mercy? Who would wish to hazard a whole eternity upon one stake? Is it not infinitely more desirable to be in a state wherein, though encompassed with infirmities, yet we do not run such a desperate risk, but if we fall we may rise again? Wherein we may say,

> *My trespass is grown up to Heaven:*
> *But far above the skies,*
> *In Christ abundantly forgiven,*
> *I see Thy mercies rise!*

In Christ! Let me entreat every serious person once more to fix his attention here. All that has been said, all that can be said, on these subjects centers in this point: the fall of Adam produced the death of Christ. Hear, O heavens, and give ear, O earth! Yea,

> *Let earth and Heaven agree,*
> *Angels and men be join'd,*
> *To celebrate with me*
> *The Saviour of mankind;*
> *T' adore the all-atoning Lamb,*
> *And bless the sound of JESUS' name!*

If God had prevented the fall of man, "the Word" had never been "made flesh"; nor had we ever "seen his glory, the glory as of the only begotten of the Father." Those mysteries never had been displayed, "which the" very "angels desire to look into." This consideration swallows up all the rest and should never be out of our thoughts. Unless "by one man judgment had come upon all men to condemnation," neither angels nor men could ever have known "the unsearchable riches of Christ."

See then, upon the whole, how little reason we have to repine at the fall of our first parent; since therefrom we may derive such unspeakable advantages, both in time and eternity. See how small pretense there is for questioning the mercy of God, in permitting that event to take place; since therein mercy, by infinite degrees, rejoices over judgment.

Where then is the man that presumes to blame God for not preventing Adam's sin? Should we not rather bless Him from the ground of the heart, for therein laying the grand scheme of man's redemption, and making way for that glorious manifestation of His wisdom, holiness, justice, and mercy? If indeed God had decreed, before the foundation of the world, that millions of men should dwell in everlasting burnings, because Adam sinned hundreds or thousands of years before they had a being, I know not who could thank Him for this, unless the devil and his angels: seeing, on this supposition, all those millions of unhappy spirits would be plunged into hell by Adam's sin, without any possible advantage from it.

But, blessed by God, this is not the case. Such a decree never existed. On the contrary, every one born of a woman may be an unspeakable gainer thereby; and none ever was or can be a loser, but by his own choice.

We see here a full answer to that plausible account of the origin of evil, published to the world some years since, and supposed to be unanswerable: that "it necessarily resulted from the nature of matter, which God was not able to alter." It is very kind in this sweet-tongued orator to make an excuse

But there is really no occasion for it: God has answered for Himself. He made man in His own image; a spirit endued with understanding and liberty. Man, abusing that liberty, produced evil;

77

brought sin and pain into the world. That God permitted, in order to a fuller manifestation of His wisdom, justice, and mercy; by bestowing on all who would receive it an infinitely greater happiness than they could possibly have attained if Adam had not fallen.

"O the depth of the riches both of the wisdom and knowledge of God!" (Romans 11:33). Although a thousand particulars of "his judgments, and of his ways, are unsearchable" to us, and past our finding out, yet may we discern the general scheme running through time into eternity. "According to the counsel of his own will," the plan He had laid before the foundation of the world, He created the parent of all mankind in His own image; and He permitted all men to be made sinners, by the disobedience of that one man, that by the obedience of one, all who receive the free gift, may be infinitely holier and happier to all eternity!

REPENTANCE

George Whitefield

(1714-1770)

George Whitefield is probably best known as an open-air preacher. He carried his own portable pulpit, from which he delivered more than 2,000 sermons in England, Wales, and America. Everywhere he went, he could draw thousands at any hour of the day. There were times when he lost all attempt at estimating the number and simply noticed how many acres they covered. But it is said his voice could be heard by as many as 30,000 people. Even these vast audiences he moved at will and made them hear except when the sound of their weeping drowned out his voice.

Not only did Whitefield preach to the common people, but to educators and philosophers as well. Benjamin Franklin was an intimate friend.

On one occasion, Whitefield was preaching in a drawing room to the aristocracy of London. He so graphically described a blind man on the verge of a precipice that the worldly Chesterfield cried out, "For heaven's sake, Whitefield, save him!"

His printed sermons may not have the best logic. But they show his ultimate goal of bringing salvation to those that heard him. This sermon on

"Repentance" is typical of his "open-air" or "field" preaching.

There is no hymn bearing Whitefield's name, but a biographer says of him, "Emotional like Charles Wesley, he yet had none of that fervid poet's music. He was nothing but a preacher. But as a preacher, he was the greatest of all his brethren, the most competent of his contemporaries being judges."

REPENTANCE

Except ye repent, ye shall all likewise perish (Luke 13:3).

WHEN WE CONSIDER how heinous and aggravating our offenses are in the sight of a just and holy God, that they bring down His wrath upon our heads, and occasion us to live under His indignation, how ought we thereby to be deterred from evil, or at least engaged to study to repent thereof, and not commit the same again!

But man is so thoughtless of an eternal state and has so little consideration of the welfare of his immortal soul, that he can sin without any thought that he must give an account of his actions at the day of judgment. Or, if he at times has any reflections on his behavior, they do not drive him to true repentance. He may for a short time refrain from falling into some gross sins that he has lately committed. But then, when the temptation comes again with power, he is carried away with the lust. And thus he goes on promising and resolving, and breaking both his resolutions and his promises as fast almost as he has made them. This is highly offensive to God; it is mocking of Him.

When grace is given us to repent truly, we shall turn wholly to God. Let me beseech you to repent of your sins, for the time is hastening when you will have neither time nor call to repent. There is none in the grave, whither we are going; but do not be afraid, for God often receives the greatest sinner to mercy through the merits of Christ Jesus. This magnifies the riches of His free grace and should be an encouragement for you who are great and notorious sinners to repent, for He will have mercy upon you if you through Christ return unto Him.

Paul was an eminent instance of this. He speaks of himself as "the chief of sinners," and he declares how God showed mercy to him. Christ loves to show mercy to sinners, and if you repent, He will have mercy on you. But as no word is more mistaken than that of repentance, I shall

1. Show you what the nature of repentance is.

2. Consider the several parts and causes of repentance.

3. I shall give you some reasons, why repentance is necessary to salvation.

4. Exhort all of you, high and low, rich and poor, one with another, to endeavor after repentance.

Repentance is the carnal and corrupt disposition of men being changed into a renewed and sanctified disposition. A man who has truly repented is truly regenerated. It is a different word for one and the same thing; the motley mixture of the beast and devil is gone. There is, as it were, a new creation wrought in your hearts. If your repentance is true, you are renewed throughout, both in soul and body; your understandings are enlightened with the knowledge of God and of the Lord Jesus Christ; and your wills, which were stubborn, obstinate, and hated all good, are obedient and conformable to the will of God.

Our deists tell us that man now has a free will to do good, to love God, and to repent when he wills. But there is no free will in any of you but to sin. Your free will leads you so far, that you would, if possible, pull God from His throne. This may, perhaps, offend the Pharisees, but (it is the truth in Christ, which I speak, I lie not) every man by his own natural will hates God. But when he is turned to the Lord by evangelical repentance, then his will is changed; then his conscience, now hardened and benumbed, shall be quickened and awakened; then his hard heart shall be melted, and his unruly affections shall be crucified. Thus, by that repentance, the whole soul will be changed, he will have new inclinations, new desires, and new habits.

You may see how vile we are by nature, that it requires a great change to be made in us to recover us from this state of sin, and therefore the consideration of our dreadful state should make us earnest with God to change our conditions, and that change true repentance implies. Therefore consider how hateful your ways are to God while you continue in sin; how abominable you are to Him while you run into evil. You cannot be said to be Christians while you are hating Christ and His people.

True repentance will entirely change you; the bias of your souls will be changed. Then you will delight in God, in Christ, in His law, and in His people. You will then believe that there is such a thing as inward feeling, though now you may esteem it madness and enthusiasm. You will not then be ashamed of becoming fools for Christ's sake; you will not regard being scoffed at. It is not then their pointing after you and crying, "Here comes another troop of His followers," will dismay you. No, your soul will abhor such proceedings; the ways of Christ and His people will be your whole delight.

It is the nature of such repentance to make a change, and the greatest change that can be made here in the soul. Thus you see what repentance implies in its own nature; it denotes an abhorrence of all evil and a forsaking of it.

Second, to show you the parts of it, and the causes concurring thereto.

The parts are sorrow, hatred, and an entire forsaking of sin.

Our sorrow and grief for sin must not spring merely from a fear of wrath. If we have no other ground but that, it proceeds from self-love and not from any love to God. If love to God is not the chief motive of your repentance, your repentance is in vain and not to be esteemed true.

Many, in our days, think their crying, "God forgive me!" or "Lord have mercy upon me!" or "I am sorry for it!" is repentance and that God will esteem it as such, but they are mistaken. It is not the drawing near to God with our lips, while our hearts are far from Him that He regards. Repentance does not come by fits and starts; it is one continued act of our lives. As we daily commit sin, so we need a daily repentance before God to obtain forgiveness for those sins we commit.

It is not your confessing yourselves to be sinners; it is not knowing your condition to be sad and deplorable, so long as you continue in your sins.

Your care and endeavors should be to get the heart thoroughly affected therewith that you may feel yourselves to be lost and undone creatures, for Christ came to save such as are lost. If you are enabled to groan under the weight and burden of your sins, then Christ will ease you and give you rest.

And till you are thus sensible of your misery and lost condition, you are a servant to sin and to your lusts, under the bondage and command of Satan, doing his drudgery. You are under the curse of God and liable to His judgment. Consider how dreadful your state will be at death and after the day of judgment when you will be exposed to such miseries that the ear has not heard, neither can the heart conceive, and that to all eternity, if you die impenitent.

But I hope better things of you though I thus speak and things that accompany salvation. Go to God in prayer, and be earnest with Him, that by His Spirit He would convince you of your miserable condition by nature and make you truly sensible thereof. Oh, be humbled, I beseech you, for your sins! Having spent so many years in sinning, what can you do less than be concerned to spend some hours in mourning and sorrowing for the same and be humbled before God?

Look back into your lives, call to mind your sins, as many as you can, the sins of your youth, as well as of your riper years. See how you have departed from a gracious Father and wandered in the way of wickedness in which you have lost yourselves, the favor of God, the comforts of His Spirit, and the peace of your own consciences. Then go and beg pardon of the Lord, through the blood of the Lamb, for the evil you have committed and for the good you have omitted.

Consider, likewise, the heinousness of your sins. See what very aggravating circumstances your sins are attended with; how you have abused the patience of God, which should have led you to repentance. When you find your heart hard, beg of God to soften it, cry mightily unto Him, and He will take away your stony heart and give you a heart of flesh.

Resolve to leave all your sinful lusts and pleasures; renounce, forsake, and abhor your old sinful course of life and serve God in holiness and righteousness all the remaining part of life. If you lament and bewail past sins and do not forsake them, your repentance is in vain. You are mocking God and deceiving your own soul; you must put off the old man with his deeds before you can put on the new man, Christ Jesus.

You, therefore, who have been swearers and cursers; you who have been harlots and drunkards; you who have been thieves and robbers; you who have hitherto followed the sinful pleasures and diversions of life, let me beseech you, by the mercies of God in Christ Jesus, that you no longer continue therein. But that you forsake your evil ways and turn to the Lord, for He waits to be gracious to you. He is ready, He is willing to pardon all your sins.

Do not expect Christ to pardon your sin when you run in it and will not abstain from complying with the temptations. But if you will be persuaded to abstain from evil and choose the good, to return unto the Lord and repent of your wickedness, He has promised He will abundantly pardon you; He will heal your backslidings and will love you freely.

Resolve now this day to have done with your sins forever. Let your old ways and you be separated; you must resolve against it, for there can be no true repentance without a resolution to forsake it. Resolve for Christ, resolve against the devil and his works, and go on fighting the Lord's battles against the devil and his emissaries; attack him in the strongest holds he has, fight him as men, as Christians, and you will soon find him to be a coward. Resist him, and he will flee from you. Resolve through grace to do this, and your repentance is half done. Then take care that you do not ground your resolutions on your own strength, but in the strength of the Lord Jesus Christ. He is the way, He is the truth, and He is the life. Without His assistance you can do nothing, but through His grace strengthening you, you will be enabled to do all things.

The more you are sensible of your own weakness and inability, the more ready Christ will be to help you; and what can all the men of the world do to you when Christ is for you? You will not regard what they say against you, for you will have the testimony of a good conscience.

Resolve to cast yourself at the feet of Christ in subjection to Him and throw yourself into the arms of Christ for salvation by Him. Consider the many invitations He has given you to come to Him, to be saved by Him. God has "laid on him the iniquity of us all."

Let me prevail with you, above all things, to make choice of the Lord Jesus Christ, resign yourselves to Him, take Him! Oh, take Him upon His own terms, and whoever you are, however great a sinner you have been, in the name of the great God do I offer Jesus Christ to you! As you value your life and soul, refuse Him not, but stir up yourself to accept the Lord Jesus, take Him wholly as He is, for He will be applied wholly to you, or else not at all. Jesus Christ must be your whole wisdom; Jesus Christ must be your whole righteousness; Jesus Christ must be your whole sanctification, or He will never be your eternal redemption.

Though you have been ever so wicked and profligate, if you will now abandon your sins and turn to the Lord Jesus Christ, you shall have Him given to you, and all your sins shall be freely forgiven. Oh, why will you neglect the great work of your repentance? Do not defer the doing of it one day longer, but today, even now, take that Christ who is freely offered to you.

Now, as to the causes hereof, the first cause is God; He is the author, "we are born of God," God has begotten us, even God, the Father of our Lord Jesus Christ. It is He who stirs us up to will and to do of His own good pleasure. Another cause is God's free grace; it is owing to the "riches of his free grace" that we have been prevented from going down to hell long ago. It is because the compassions of the Lord fail not; they are new every morning and fresh every morning.

Sometimes the instruments are very unlikely. A poor despised minister or member of Jesus Christ may, by the power of God, be an instrument in the hands of God to bring you to true evangelical repentance. This may be done to show that the power is not in men, but that it is entirely owing to the good pleasure of God.

If there has been any good done among you by preaching the Word, as I trust there has, though it were preached in a field, if God has met and owned us and blessed His Word, though preached by an enthusiastic babbler, a boy, a madman, I do rejoice, yea, and will rejoice, let foes say what they will.

Third, I shall show the reasons why repentance is necessary to salvation.

And that is plainly revealed to us in the Word of God. The soul that does not repent and turn to the Lord shall die in its sins, and their blood shall be required at their own hands. It is necessary, as we have sinned, we should repent; for a holy God could not, nor even can, or will, admit anything that is unholy into His presence.

This is the beginning of grace in the soul. There must be a change in heart and life before there can be a dwelling with a holy God. You cannot love sin and God too; you cannot love God and mammon. No unclean person can stand in the presence of God; it is contrary to the holiness of His nature. There is a contrariety between the holy nature of God and the unholy nature of carnal and unregenerate men.

What communication can there be between a sinless God and creatures full of sin, between a pure God and impure creatures? If you were to be admitted into heaven with your present tempers in your impenitent condition, heaven itself would be a hell to you. The songs of angels would be as enthusiasm and would be intolerable to you.

Therefore you must have those tempers changed; you must be as holy as God. He must be your God here, and you must be His people, or you will never dwell together in all eternity. If you hate the ways of God and cannot spend an hour in His service, how will you be easy in all eternity, in singing praises to Him who sits upon the throne and to the Lamb forever?

And that is to be the employment of all those who are admitted into this glorious place, where neither sin nor sinner is admitted, where no scoffer ever can come, without repentance from his evil ways, a turning to God, and a cleaving to Him. That must be done before any can be admitted into the glorious mansions of God, which are prepared for all who love the Lord Jesus Christ in sincerity and truth. Repent then of all your sins!

It makes my blood run cold to think that any of you might not be admitted into the glorious mansions above. Oh, that it were in my power, I would place you, yea, you my scoffing friend, and the greatest enemy I have on earth, at the right hand of Jesus, but that I cannot do. However, I advise and exhort you, with all love and tenderness, to make Jesus your refuge. Flee to Him for relief! Jesus died to save such as you; He is full of compassion. If you go to Him as poor, lost, undone sinners, Jesus will give you His Spirit; you shall live and reign, and reign and live, you shall love and live, and live and love, with this Jesus to all eternity.

Fourth, I exhort you, high and low, rich and poor, one with another, to repent all of your sins and turn to the Lord.

And I shall speak to each of you. You have either repented, or you have not; you are believers in Christ Jesus or unbelievers.

And first, you who never have truly repented of your sins and never have truly forsaken your lusts, be not offended if I speak plainly to you; for it is love, love to your souls, that constrains me to speak.

I shall lay before you your danger and the misery to which you are exposed while you remain impenitent in sin. And, oh, that this may be a means of making you flee to Christ for pardon and forgiveness!

While your sins are not repented of, you are in danger of death; and if you should die, you would perish forever. There is no hope of any who live and die in their sins, but that they will dwell with devils and damned spirits to all eternity. And how do we know we shall live much longer? We are not sure of seeing our own habitations this night in safety.

What do you mean then, being at ease and pleasure while your sins are not pardoned? As sure as ever the Word of God is true, if you die in that condition, you are shut out of all hope and mercy forever and shall pass into easeless and endless misery.

What are all your pleasures and diversions worth? They last but for a moment, they are of no worth, and but of short continuance. And sure it must be gross folly, eagerly to pursue those sinful lusts and pleasures that war against the soul, that tend to harden the heart and keep us from closing with the Lord Jesus. Indeed, they are destructive of our peace here and, without repentance, will be of our peace hereafter.

Oh, the folly and madness of this sensual world! If there were nothing in sin but present slavery, it would keep an ingenuous spirit from it. But to do the devil's drudgery! If we do that, we shall have his wages—eternal death and condemnation. Oh, consider this, you who think it no crime to swear, whore, drink, or scoff and jeer at the people of God!

Repentance

Consider how your voices will then be changed, and you, that counted your lives madness and your end without honor, shall howl and lament at your own madness and folly that brought you to so much woe and distress. Then you will lament and bemoan your own dreadful condition, but it will be of no signification; for He who is now your merciful Savior will then become your inexorable judge. Now He is easy to be entreated; but then, all your tears and prayers will be in vain. For God has allotted to every man a day of grace, a time of repentance, which, if he does not improve, but neglects and despises the means that are offered to him, he cannot be saved.

Therefore, while you continue in a course of sin and unrighteousness, I beseech you to think of the consequence that will attend the misspending of your precious time. Your souls are worth being concerned about! For if you can enjoy all the pleasures and diversions of life, at death you must leave them; that will put an end to all your worldly concerns. And will it not be very deplorable to have your good things here all over—all your earthly, sensual, devilish pleasures with which you have been taken up? The thought for how trifling a concern you have lost eternal welfare will gnaw your very soul.

Your wealth and grandeur will stand in no stead; you can carry nothing of it into the other world. Then the consideration of your uncharitableness to the poor, and the ways you take to obtain your wealth will be a very hell to you.

Now you enjoy the means of grace, the preaching of His Word, prayer, and sacraments; and God has sent His ministers out into the fields and highways to invite, to woo you to come in. But they are tiresome to you; you would rather be at your pleasures. Soon they will be over, and you will be no more troubled with them; but then you would give ten thousand worlds for one moment of that merciful time of grace that you have abused. Then you will cry for a drop of that precious blood that now you trample under your feet. Then you will wish for one more offer of mercy, for Christ and His free grace to be offered to you again.

But your crying will be in vain, for as you would not repent here, God will not give you an opportunity to repent hereafter. If you would not in Christ's time, you shall not in your own time. In what a dreadful condition will you then be? What horror and astonishment will possess your souls?

Then all your lies and oaths, your scoffs and jeers at the people of God, all your filthy and unclean thoughts and actions, your misspent time in ballrooms and theaters, your whole evenings at cards, dice, and taverns, your worldliness, covetousness, and uncharitableness will be brought to your remembrance and at once charged upon your guilty soul.

And how can you bear the thoughts of these things? Indeed, I am full of compassion toward you to think that this should be the portion of any of you. These are truths, though awful ones; these are the truths of the gospel. If there were not a necessity for thus speaking, I would willingly forbear, for it is a no more pleasing subject to me than it is to you.

But it is my duty to show you the dreadful consequences of continuing in sin. I am only now acting the part of a skillful surgeon who searches a wound before he heals it. I would show you your danger first, that deliverance may be the more readily accepted by you.

Consider, that however you may be for putting the evil day away from you, and are now striving to hide your sins, at the day of judgment there shall be a full discovery of all.

Hidden things on that day shall be brought to light; and after all your sins have been revealed to the whole world, then you must depart into everlasting fire in hell, which will not be quenched night and day; it will be without intermission, without end. What stupidity and senselessness has possessed your hearts that you are not frightened from your sins? The fear of Nebuchadnezzar's fiery furnace made men do anything to avoid it; and shall not an everlasting fire make men, make you, do anything to avoid it?

Oh, that this would awaken and cause you to humble yourselves for your sins and to beg pardon for them that you might find mercy in the Lord!

Let me beseech you to cast away your transgressions, to strive against sin, to watch against it, and to beg power and strength from Christ, to keep down the power of those lusts that hurry you on in your sinful ways.

But if you will not do any of these things, if you are resolved to sin on, you must expect eternal death to be the consequence. You must expect to be seized with horror and trembling, with horror and amazement, to hear the dreadful sentence of condemnation pronounced against you. Then you will run and call upon the mountains to fall on you to hide you from the Lord and from the fierce anger of His wrath.

Had you now a heart to turn from your sins to the living God by true and unfeigned repentance, and to pray to Him for mercy in and through the merits of Jesus Christ, there were hope. But at the day of judgment your prayers and tears will be of no significance; they will be of no service to you. The judge will not be entreated by you. As you would not hearken to Him when He called to you, but despised both Him and His ministers, and would not leave your iniquities, therefore on that day He will not be entreated, notwithstanding all your cries and tears.

God Himself has said: "Because I have called and ye refused; I have stretched out my hand, and no man regarded; But ye have set at nought all my counsel, and would none of my reproof: I also will laugh at your calamity; I will mock when your fear cometh . . . as desolation, and your destruction cometh as a whirlwind; when distress and anguish cometh upon you. Then shall they call upon me, but I will not answer; they shall seek me early, but they shall not find me" (Proverbs 1:24-28).

Now, you may call this enthusiasm and madness. But at that great day, if you repent not of your sins here, you will find that your own ways were madness indeed. But God forbid that it should be left undone till then! Seek after the Lord while He is to be found; call upon Him while He is near, and you shall find mercy. Repent this hour, and Christ will joyfully receive you.

What say you? Must I go to my Master and tell Him you will not come to Him and will have none of His counsels? No; do not send me on so unhappy an errand. I cannot, I will not tell Him any such thing. Shall not I rather tell Him that you are willing to repent and to be converted, to become new men and take up a new course of life? That is the only wise resolution you can make. Let me tell my Master that you will come to Him and will wait upon Him, for if you do not, it will be your ruin in time and eternity.

You will at death wish you had lived the life of the righteous, that you might have died his death. Be advised then! Consider what is before you, Christ and the world, holiness and sin, life and death. Choose now for yourselves; let your choice be made immediately, and let that choice be your dying choice.

If you would not choose to die in your sins, to die drunkards, to die adulterers, to die swearers and scoffers, live not this night in your dreadful condition. Some of you may say you have no power, you have no strength; but have not you been wanting to yourselves in such things that were within your power? Have you not as much power to go to hear a sermon as to go into a theater or to a dance? You have as much power to read the Bible as to read plays, novels, and romances. You can associate as well with the godly as with the wicked and profane. This is but an idle excuse to go on in your sins.

If you will be found in the means of grace, Christ has promised He will give you strength. While Peter was preaching, the Holy Ghost fell on all that heard the word. How then should you be found in the way of your duty! Jesus Christ will then give you strength; He will put His Spirit within you; you shall find He will be your wisdom, your righteousness, your sanctification, and your redemption. See what a gracious, kind, and loving Master He is ! He will be a help in all your burdens, and if the burden of sin be on your soul, go to Him as weary and heavy-laden, and you shall find rest.

Do not say your sins are too many and too great to expect to find mercy. No; be they ever so many or ever so great, the blood of the Lord Jesus Christ will cleanse you from all sins. God's grace is free, rich, and sovereign.

Manasseh was a great sinner, and yet he was pardoned. Zaccheus was far from God and went to see Christ only to satisfy his curiosity, and yet Jesus met him and brought salvation to his house. Manasseh was a idolater and murderer, yet he received mercy. Another was an oppressor and extortioner who had gotten riches by fraud and deceit, and by grinding the faces of the poor. So did Matthew too, and yet they both found mercy.

Have you been blasphemers and persecutors of the saints and servants of God? So was Paul. Yet he received mercy. Have you been a thief? The thief upon the cross found mercy. I despair of none of you, however vile and profligate you have been. I say, I despair of none of you, especially when God has had mercy on such a wretch as I am.

Remember the publican, how he found favor with God, when the proud, self-conceited Pharisee, who, puffed up with his own righteousness, was rejected. And if you will go to Jesus as the publican did, under a sense of your own unworthiness, you shall find favor as he did. There is virtue enough in the blood of Jesus to pardon greater sinners than He has yet pardoned. Then be not discouraged, but come to Jesus, and you will find Him ready to help in all your distresses, to lead you into all truth, to bring you from darkness to light, and from the power of Satan to God.

Repentance

Do not let the devil deceive you by telling you that then all your delights and pleasures will be over. No; rather than depriving you of all pleasure it is an inlet into unspeakable delights, peculiar to all who are truly regenerated. The new birth is the very beginning of a life of peace and comfort; and the greatest pleasantness is to be found in the ways of holiness.

Solomon, who had experience of all other pleasures, yet said of the ways of godliness, "That all her ways are ways of pleasantness, and all her paths are paths of peace." Then surely you will not let the devil deceive you. It is all he wants; it is that he aims at, to make religion appear to be melancholy, miserable, and enthusiastic. But let him say what he will, give not ear to him, regard him not, for he always was and will be a liar.

What words, what entreaties shall I use to make you come to the Lord Jesus Christ? The little love I have experienced since I have been brought from sin to God is so great that I would not be in a natural state for ten thousand worlds, and what I have felt is but little to what I hope to feel. But that little love that I have experienced is a sufficient buoy against all the storms and tempests of this boisterous world. Let men and devils do their worst. I rejoice in the Lord Jesus. Yea, and I will rejoice.

And if you repent and come to Jesus, I would rejoice on your account too. We should rejoice together to all eternity, when once on the other side of the grave. Come to Jesus! The arms of Jesus Christ will embrace you; He will wash away all your sins in His blood and will love you freely.

Come, I beseech you; come to Jesus Christ! Oh, that my words would pierce to the very soul! Oh,

97

that Jesus Christ were formed in you! That you would turn to the Lord Jesus Christ that He might have mercy on you!

I would speak till I could speak no more, so it might be a means to bring you to Jesus. Let the Lord Jesus Christ enter your souls, and you shall find peace that the world can neither give nor take away. There is mercy for the greatest sinner among you. Go to the Lord as sinners, helpless and undone, and you shall find comfort to your souls and be admitted at last among those who sing praises to the Lord to all eternity.

Now let me speak a word of exhortation to those of you who are born again, who belong to God, who have repented of your sins and are cleansed from their guilt, and that is, Be thankful to God for His mercies toward you. Admire the grace of God, and bless His name forever! Are you made alive in Christ Jesus? Is the life of God begun in your souls, and have you the evidence thereof? Be thankful for this unspeakable mercy to you. Never forget to speak of His mercy.

And as your life was formerly devoted to sin and to the pleasures of the world, let it now be spent wholly in the ways of God, and embrace every opportunity of doing and of receiving good. Whatever opportunity you have, do it vigorously, do it speedily, do not defer it. If you see one hurrying on to destruction, use the utmost of your endeavor to stop him in his course. Show him the need he has of repentance and that without it he is lost forever. Do not regard his despising of you; still go on to show him his danger. If your friends mock and despise, do not let that discourage you. Hold on; hold out to the end, so you shall have a crown that is immutable and that fades not away.

Let the love of Jesus to you keep you also humble. Do not be high-minded; keep close to the Lord; observe the rules that the Lord Jesus Christ has given in His Word, and let not the instructions be lost that you are capable of giving. Consider what reason you have to be thankful to the Lord Jesus Christ for giving you that repentance you yourselves had need of; a repentance that works by love.

Now you find more pleasure in walking with God one hour than in all your former carnal delights and all the pleasures of sin. Oh, the joy you feel in your own souls, which all the men of this world, and all the devils in hell though they were to combine together, could not destroy. Then fear not their wrath or malice, for through many tribulations we must enter into glory.

A few days, or weeks, or years more, and then you will be beyond their reach. You will be in the heavenly Jerusalem; there is all harmony and love; there is all joy and delight; there the weary is at rest.

Now we have many enemies, but at death they are all lost; they cannot follow us beyond the grave. That is a great encouragement to us not to regard the scoffs and jeers of the men of this world.

Let the love of Jesus be in your thoughts continually. It was His death that brought you life; it was His crucifixion that paid the satisfaction for your sins; His death, burial, and resurrection that completed the work; and He is now in heaven, interceding for you at the right hand of His Father.

And can you do too much for the Lord Jesus Christ, who has done so much for you? His love to you is unfathomable. Oh, the height, the depth, the length, and breadth of that love that brought the King of glory from His throne to die for such rebels as we are, when we had acted so unkindly against Him and deserved nothing but eternal damnation! He came down and took our nature upon Him; He was made of flesh and dwelt among us; He was put to death on our account; He paid our ransom. Surely that should make us love the Lord Jesus Christ; should make us rejoice in Him and not do as too many have done, and as we ourselves have too often done, crucify this Jesus afresh. Let us do all we can to honor Him.

Come, all of you, and behold Him stretched out for you. See His hands and fel for you! Can you think of a panting, bleeding, dying Jesus and not be filled with pity toward Him? He underwent all that for you. Come to Him by faith; lay hold on Him; there is mercy for every soul that will come to Him. Then do not delay; flee to the arms of this Jesus, and you shall be made clean in His blood.

What shall I say to you to make you come to Jesus? I have showed you the dreadful consequences of not repenting of your sins; and if, after all I have said, you are resolved to persist, your blood will be required at your own hands. But I hope better things of you, and things that accompany salvation. Let me beg of you to pray in good earnest for the grace of repentance.

I may never see your faces again, but at the day of judgment I will meet you. There you will either bless God that you were moved to repentance, or else this sermon will be a swift witness against you. Repent, therefore, as John the Baptist and our

Repentance

blessed Redeemer Himself earnestly exhorted, and turn from your evil ways. The Lord will have mercy on you.

FURY NOT IN GOD

Thomas Chalmers

(1780-1847)

Thomas Chalmers was a leader in the Free Church of Scotland. Though he was licensed to preach in 1799, it was not until 1811, following the death of his sister, that Chalmers had a deep religious experience that changed his life.

In addition to holding several pastorates he was professor of theology at the University of Edinburgh as well as moderator of the Church of Scotland. He was a proponent of the growing spirit of evangelism and revival in the church. He held the right of the church to choose its own minister and front leader of the protesting party in the church and state controversy. When the state refused these rights, he led about a third of the ministers of the church out of the General Assembly in 1842 and 1843 that resulted in the Free Church of Scotland. He became the principal and professor of the newly founded Free Church College in Edinburgh, a position he held until his death.

Chalmers was one of the greatest preachers of the age. It is said that next to Knox stands Chalmers. Like Knox, he was especially great in the pulpit and was one of the most eminent and practical pastors of his age or any age.

Among the best and most famous sermons were his "Astronomical Discourses" and "The Expulsive Power of a New Affection." His favorite sermon however was:

FURY NOT IN GOD

Fury is not in me: who would set the briers and thorns against me in battle? I would go through them, I would burn them together. Or let him take hold of my strength, that he may make peace with me; and he shall make peace with me (Isaiah 27:4-5).

THERE ARE THREE distinct lessons in this text. The first, that fury is not in God; the second, that He does not want to glorify Himself by the death of sinners—"Who would set the thorns and briers against me in battle?"; the third, the invitation—"Take hold of my strength, that you may make peace with me; and you shall make peace with me."

First, then, fury is not in God. But how can this be? Is not fury one manifestation of His essential attributes? Do we not repeatedly read of His fury—of Jerusalem's being full of the fury of the Lord—of God's casting the fury of His wrath upon the world—of His rendering His anger upon His enemies with fury—of His accomplishing His fury upon Zion—of His causing His fury to rest on the bloody and devoted city?

We are not therefore to think that fury is banished altogether from God's administration. There are times and occasions when this fury is discharged upon the objects of it; and there must be other times and other occasions when there is no fury in

Him. Now what is the occasion upon which He disclaims all fury in our text? He is inviting men to reconciliation; He is calling upon them to make peace; and He is assuring them that if they will only take hold of His strength, they shall make peace with Him.

In the preceding verses He speaks of a vineyard and in the act of inviting people to lay hold of His strength. He is in fact inviting those who are without the limits of the vineyard to enter in. Fury will be discharged on those who reject the invitation. But we cannot say that there is any exercise of fury in God at the time of giving the invitation. There is the most visible and direct contrary. There is a longing desire after you. There is a wish to save you from that day in which the fury of a rejected Savior will be spread abroad over all who have despised Him. The tone of invitation is not a tone of anger—it is a tone of tenderness. The look that accompanies the invitation is not a look of wrath—it is a look of affection.

There may be a time, there may be an occasion, when the fury of God will be put forth on the men who have held out against Him and turned them away in infidelity and contempt from His beseeching voice; but at the time that He is lifting this voice—at the time that He is sending messengers over the face of the earth to circulate it among the habitations of men—at the time particularly among ourselves, when in our own place and our own day Bibles are within the reach of every family, and ministers in every pulpit are sounding forth the overtures of the gospel throughout the land—surely at such a time and upon such an occasion it may well be said of God to all who are now seeking His face and favor that there is no fury in Him.

It is just as in the parable of the marriage feast. Many rejected the invitation that the king gave the people—for which he was angry with them, sent forth his armies, destroyed them, and burned up their city. On that occasion there was fury in the king, and on the like occasion will there be fury in God. But well can He say at the time when He is now giving the invitation—"there is no fury in Me." There is kindness—a desire for peace and friendship—a longing earnestness to make up the quarrel that now subsists between the Lawgiver in heaven and His yet impenitent and unreconciled creatures.

That very process was all gone through at and before the destruction of Jerusalem. It rejected the warnings and invitations of the Savior and at length experienced His fury. But there was no fury at the time of His giving the invitations. The tone of our Savior's voice when He uttered, "O Jerusalem, Jerusalem," was not the tone of a vindictive and irritated fury. There was compassion in it—a warning and pleading earnestness that they would mind the things that belong to their peace. At that time when He would willingly have gathered them as a hen gathereth her chickens under her wings—then may it well be said that there was no fury in the Son of God, no fury in God.

Let us make the application to ourselves in the present day. On the last day there will be a tremendous discharge of fury. That wrath that sinners are now doing so much to treasure up will all be poured forth on them. The season of God's mercy will then have come to an end; and after the sound of the last trumpet, there will never more be heard the sounding call of reconciliation. Oh, that God, who is grieved and who is angry with sinners every day, will in the last day pour it all forth in one mighty torrent on the heads of the unrepentent. It is now gathering and accumulating in a storehouse of vengeance; and at the awful point in the successive history of nature and providence, when time shall be no more, will the door of this storehouse be opened, that the fury of the Lord may break loose upon the guilty and accomplish upon them the weight and the terror of all His threatenings.

You misunderstand the text if you infer from it that fury has no place in the history or methods of God's administration. It has its time and its occasion, and the very greatest display of it is yet to come, when the earth shall be burned up and the heavens shall be dissolved, the elements shall melt with fervent heat,"and the Lord Jesus shall be revealed from heaven with His mighty angels in flaming fire taking vengeance on them that know not God, and obey not the gospel of our Lord Jesus Christ: who shall be punished with everlasting destruction from the presence of the Lord, and from the glory of His power" (2 Thessalonians 1:7-9). It makes one shudder to think that there may be some here whom this devouring torrent of wrath shall sweep away; some here who will be drawn into the whirl of destruction and forced to take their descending way through the mouth of that pit where the worm dieth not and the fire is not quenched; some here who, so far from experiencing in their own persons that there is no fury in God, will find that throughout the dreary extent of one hopeless and endless and unmitigated eternity, it is the only attribute of His they have to do with.

But hear me, hear me before you have taken your

bed in hell; hear me before that prison door be shut upon you that is never, never again to be opened! Hear me, hear me, before the great day of the revelation of God's wrath comes round, and there shall be a total breaking up of that sytem of things that looks at present so stable and so unalterable! On that awful day I might not be able to take up the text and say that there is no fury in God. But, oh, hear me, for your lives, hear me—on this day I can say it. From the place where I now stand I can announce to you that there is no fury in God; and there is not one of you into whose heart this announcement may not enter. Welcome will you be to enter with your beseeching God a league of peace and of friendship that shall never be broken asunder.

Surely when I am holding out the language of entreaty, sounding in your ears the tidings of gladness, and inviting you to enter into the vineyard of God—surely at that time I may well say that there is no fury in God.

Surely at the time when the Son of God is inviting you to enter into reconciliation, there is neither the feeling nor the exercise of fury. It is only if you refuse, if you persist in refusing, and if you allow all those calls and entreaties to be lost upon you, it is only then that God will execute His fury and put forth the power of His anger. Therefore He says to us, "Kiss the Son, lest He be angry, and ye perish from the way, when His wrath is kindled but a little" (Psalm 2:12). Such then is the interesting point of time at which you stand. There is no fury in God at the very time that He is inviting you to flee from it. He is sending forth no blasting influence upon the fig tree, even though hitherto it had borne no

---

fruit and been a mere cumberer of the ground. He says, We shall let it alone for another year, and dig it, and dress it, and if it bear fruit, well; and if not, then let it be afterward cut down (Luke 13:8-9). You are all in the situation of this fig tree; you are for the present let alone. God has purposes of kindness toward every one of you. As one of His ministers, I can now say to you all that there is no fury in Him.

Now when the spiritual husbandman is trying to soften your hearts he is warranted to make full use of the argument of my text—that there is no fury in God. Now that the ambassador of Christ is plying you with the offers of grace and strength to renew and to make you fruitful He is surely charged with matter of far different import from wrath and threatening and vengeance. Oh, let not all this spiritual husbandry turn out to be unavailing; let not the offer be made now and no fruit appear afterwards. Let not yours be the fate of the barren and unfruitful fig tree.

The day of the fury of the Lord is approaching. The burning up of this earth and the passing away of these heavens is an event in the history of God's administration to which we are continually drawing nearer. On that day when the whole of universal nature shall be turned into a heap of ruins we shall see the gleam of a mighty conflagration, shall hear the noise of the framework of creation rending into fragments, and a cry shall be raised from a despairing multitude out of the men of all generations who have just awakened from their resting places—and amid all the bustle and consternation that is going on below, such a sight shall be witnessed from the canopy of heaven as will spread silence over the face of the world and fix and solemnize every individual of its incumbent population.

Let us not think that on that day when the Judge is to appear, charged with the mighty object of vindicating before men and angels the truth and majesty of God, that the fury of God will not then appear in bright and burning manifestation. But what I have to tell you on this day is that fury is not in God—that now is the time of those things that belong to the peace of our eternity; and that if you will only hear on this the day of your merciful visitation, you will be carried off in safety from all those horrors of dissolving nature. Amid the wild war and frenzy of its reeling elements you will be carried by the arms of love to a place of security and everlasting triumph.

That brings us to the second head of discourse: God is not wanting to glorify Himself by the death of sinners. "Who would set the briers and thorns against me in battle?" The wicked and the righteous are often represented in Scripture by figures taken from the vegetable world. The saved and sanctified are called trees of righteousness, the planting of the Lord that He might be glorified. The godly man is said to be like a tree planted by the rivers of water that brings forth its fruit in its season. The judgment that comes upon a man is compared to an axe laid to the root of a tree. A tree is said to be known by its fruit; and as a proof that the kind of character of men is specified by the kind of tree in the woods, we read that of thorns men do not gather figs nor of the bramble bush gather they grapes. You will observe that the thorn is one of the kinds instanced in the text, and when God says, "I would go through them, I would burn them together," He speaks of the destruction that comes on all who remain in the state of thorns and briers. That agrees with what we read in the epistle to the Hebrews, "That which beareth thorns and briers is rejected, and is nigh unto cursing; whose end is to be burned" (Hebrews 6:8).

Thorns and briers are in other places still more directly employed to signify the enemies of God. "And the light of Israel shall be for a fire," says one of the prophets, "and His Holy One for a flame, and it shall burn and devour His thorns and His briers in one day." Therefore when God says in the text, "Who would set the briers and thorns against me in battle? I would go through them, I would burn them together," He speaks of the ease wherewith He could accomplish His wrath upon His enemies. They would perish before Him like the moth. They could not stand the lifting up of the red right arm of the displeasure of Almighty God.

Why set up a contest so unequal as this? Why put the wicked in battle array against Him who could go through them and devour them in an instant by the breath of His fury? God is saying in the text that that is not what He is wanting. He does not want to set Himself forth as an enemy or as a strong man armed against them for the battle; it is a battle He is not at all disposed to enter into. The glory He would achieve by a victory over a host so feeble is not a glory that His heart is at all set upon.

Oh, no, ye children of men. He has no pleasure in your death; He is not seeking to magnify Himself by the destruction of so paltry a foe. He could devour you in a moment; He could burn you up like stubble. You mistake it if you think that renown on so poor a field of contest is a renown that He is aspiring after. Who would set the grasshoppers in battle array against the giants? Who would set thorns and briers in battle array against God? That is not what He wants; He would rather something else.

Be assured that He would rather you were to turn, live, come into His vineyard, submit to the regenerating power of His spiritual husbandry, and be changed from the nature of an accursed plant to a tree of righteousness. In the language of the next verse, He would rather that this enemy of His, not yet at peace with Him, who may therefore be likened to a brier or a thorn—He would rather that he remained so that he should take hold of God's strength, that he may make peace with Him—and as the fruit of his so doing, he shall make peace with Him.

Now tell me if that does not open up a most wonderful and a most inviting view of God? It is the real attitude in which He puts Himself forth to us in the gospel of His Son. He there says, in the hearing of all to whom the word of this salvation is sent, "Why will ye die?"

It is true that by your death He could manifest the dignity of His Godhead; He could make known the power of His wrath; He could spread the awe of His truth and His majesty over the whole territory of His government and send forth to its uttermost limits the glories of His strength and His immutable sovereignty. But He does not want to magnify Himself over you in this way; He has no ambition whatever after the renown of such a victory over such weak and insignificant enemies. Their resistance was no trial whatever to His strength or to His greatness. There is nothing in the destruction of creatures so weak that can at all bring Him any distinction or throw any aggrandizement around Him. In Scripture everywhere do we see Him pleading and protesting that He does not want to signalize Himself upon the ruin of any but would rather that they should turn and be saved.

And now what remains for you to do? God is willing to save you. Are you willing to be saved? The way is set before you most patiently and clearly in the Bible. The very text, brief as it is, points out to you the way, as I shall endeavor to explain and set before you in the third head of discourse. But meanwhile, and all the better to secure a hearing from you, let me ask you to lay it upon your consciences whether you are in a state that will do for you to die in. If not, then I beseech you to think how certainly death will, and how speedily it may, come upon the likeliest of you all.

The very youngest among you know very well that if not cut off previously—which is a very possible thing—then manhood will come. Old age will come, the dying bed will come, and the very last look you shall ever cast on your acquaintances will come. The agony of the parting breath will come, the time when you are stretched a lifeless corpse before the eyes of weeping relatives will come, the coffin that is to enclose you will come, and that hour when the company assemble to carry you to the churchyard will come. That minute when you are put into the grave will come, and the throwing in of the loose earth into the narrow house where you are laid and the spreading of the green sod over it. All, all will come on every living creature who now hears me. In a few little years the minister who now speaks and the people who now listen will be carried to their graves to make room for another generation.

Now all this must and will happen; your common sense and common experience serve to convince you of it. Perhaps it may have been little thought of in the days of careless, thoughtless, and thankless concern that you have spent thus far; but I call upon you to think of it now, to lay it seriously to heart, and no longer to trifle and delay, when the high matters of death and judgment and eternity are set before you.

The tidings with which I am charged—and the blood lies upon your own head and not upon mine if you will not listen to them—the object of my coming among you is to let you know what more things are to come. It is to carry you beyond the regions of sight and of sense to the regions of faith, and to assure you, in the name of Him who cannot lie, that as sure as the hour of laying the body in the grave comes, so surely will also come the hour of the spirit returning to the God who gave it. Yes, and the day of final reckoning will come. The appearance of the Son of God in heaven, His mighty angels around Him, the opening of the books, the standing of the men of all generations before the judgment seat, the solemn passing of that sentence that is to fix you for eternity will come. Yes, and if you refuse to be reconciled in the name of Christ, now that He is beseeching you to be so, if you refuse to turn from the evil of your ways and to do and to be what your Savior would have you, I must tell you what that sentence is to be: "Depart from me, ye cursed, into everlasting fire, prepared for the devil and his angels."

Fury Not in God

There is a way of escape from the fury of this tremendous storm. There is a pathway of egress from the state of condemnation to the state of acceptance. There is a method pointed out in Scripture by which we, who by nature are the children of wrath, may come to be at peace with God. Let all ears be open then to our explanation of this way, as we bid you in the language of our text to take hold of God's strength that you may make peace with Him. If you do, you shall make peace with Him.

Read now the fifth verse: "Or let him take hold of my strength, that he may make peace with me; and he shall make peace with me." "Or" here is the same with "rather." Rather than that what is spoken of in the fourth verse should fall upon you, rather than that I should engage in battle with mine enemies, rather than that a result so melancholy to them should take place, as my going through them and burning them together—rather than that all this should happen, I would greatly prefer that they took hold of my strength in order to make peace with me. I promise, as the sure effect of this proceeding, that they shall make peace with me.

We have not far to seek for what is meant by this strength, for Isaiah himself speaks (chapter 33:6) of the strength of salvation. It is not your destruction but your salvation that God wants to put forth His strength in.

There has strength been already put forth in the deliverance of a guilty world—the very strength that He wants you to lay hold of. He will be glorified in the destruction of the sinner, but He would like better to be glorified by his salvation. To destroy you is to do no more than to set fire to briers and thorns and to consume them; but to save you—

this is indeed the power of God and the wisdom of God—this is the mighty achievement that angels desire to look into—this is the enterprise upon which a mighty Captain embarked all the energy that belonged to Him and traveled in the greatness of His strength until He accomplished it. Now that it is accomplished, God would much rather be glorified in the salvation of His saints than glorified in the destruction of sinners (2 Thessalonians 1:7,10).

God will show His wrath and make His power known in the destruction of the sinner. But it is a more glorious work of power to redeem that sinner, and this He engages to do for you if you will take hold of His strength. He would greatly prefer this way of making His power known. He does not want to enter into battle with you or to consume you like stubble by the breath of His indignation. No, He wants to transform sinners into saints; He wants to transform vessels of wrath into vessels of mercy and to make known the riches of His glory on those whom He had previously prepared unto glory.

There is a strength put forth in the destruction of the sinner, but there is also a strength put forth in the salvation of a sinner. This is the strength that He wants you to lay hold of in my text. This is the strength by the display of which He would prefer being glorified. He would rather decline entering into a contest with you sinners; for to gain a victory over you would be no more to Him than to fight with the briers and the thorns and to consume them. From enemies He wants to make friends of you; from the children of wrath to transform you into the children of adoption; from the state of guilt to accomplish such a mighty and a wonderful change upon you, as to put you into the state of justification; from the servants of sin to make you in the day of His power the willing servants of God; to chase away from your faculties the darkness of nature and to make all light and comfort around you; to turn you from a slave of sense and to invest with all their rightful ascendency over your affections the things of eternity; to pull down the strongholds of corruption within you and raise him who was spiritually dead to a life of new obedience. This is the victory over you which God aspires after. It is your thorough and complete salvation from the punishment of sin and the power of sin on which He is desirous of exalting the glory of His strength. This is the strength that He calls you to take hold upon.

Let me now say a few more things about this strength, the strength of salvation that is spoken of in the text, and then state very briefly what it is to lay hold upon.

First we read of a mighty strength that had to be put forth in the work of a sinner's justification. You know that all men are sinners, and so all are under the righteous condemnation of God. How, in the name of all that is difficult and wonderful, can these sinners ever get this condemnation removed from them? By what new and unheard-of process can the guilty before God ever again become justified in His sight? How from that throne, of which it is said that judgment and justice are the habitation, can the sentence of acquittal ever be heard on the children of iniquity?

How can God's honor be kept entire in the sight of angels if we men who have repeatedly mocked Him and insulted Him, and made our own wish and our own way take the precedency of His high and solemn requirements—if we, with all this contempt of the Lawgiver expressed in our lives and all this character of rebellion against Him written upon our foreheads shall be admitted to a place of distinction in heaven—and that too after God has committed Himself in the hearing of angels—after He had given us a law by the disposition of angels, and we had not kept it—and after He had said how the wicked shall not go unpunished, but that cursed is every one who continues not in all words of the book of God's law to do them? But what is more, it was not merely the good and the obedient angels who knew our rebellion. The malignant and fallen angels not only knew it, but they devised and they promoted it. And how, I would ask, can God keep the awful majesty of His truth and justice entire in the sight of His adversaries if Satan and the angels of wickedness along with him shall have it in their power to say they prevailed on man to insult Him by sin and have compelled God to put up with the affront and to connive at it?

Now, just in proportion to the weight and magnitude of the obstacle was the greatness of that strength that the Savior put forth in the mighty work of moving it away. We have no adequate conception upon this matter and must just take our lesson from revelation about it. Whether we take the prophecies that foretold the work of our Redeemer, or the history that relates it, or the doctrine that expounds on its worth and its efficacy— all go to establish that there was the operation of a power, that there was the severity of a conflict, that there was the high undertaking of an arduous and mighty warfare, that there were all the throes and all the exertions of a struggling, and at length a prevailing energy in the execution of that work that our Savior had to do. He had a barrier to surmount, and that too with the cries and the pains and the sorrows of heavy suffering and labor. A mighty obstacle lay before Him, and He, in the business of removing it, had to travel in all the greatness of the faculties that belonged to Him. There was a burden laid upon His shoulders that no one else but the Prince of Peace could have borne. There was a task put into His hand that none but He could fulfill.

And had the question ever been reasoned throughout the hosts of paradise: Who can so bend the unchangeable attributes of God, who can give them a shift so wonderful that the sinners who have insulted Him may be taken into forgiveness, and His honor be kept untainted and entire?—there is not one of the mighty throng who would not have shrunk from an enterprise so lofty. There is not one of them who could at once magnify the law and release man from its violated sanctions. There is not one of them who could turn its threatening away from us and at the same time give to the truth and the justice of God their brightest manifestation. There is not one of them who could unravel the mystery of our redemption through all the difficulties that beset and surround it. There is not one of them who, by the strength of his arm, could have obtained conquest over these difficulties.

However little we may enter into the elements of this weighty speculation, let us forget not that the question was not merely between God and man. It was between God and all the creatures He had formed. They saw the dilemma; they felt how deeply it involved the character of the deity; they

119

perceived its every bearing on the majesty of His attributes and on the stability of the government that was upheld by Him. With them it was a matter of deep and most substantial interest. When the Eternal Son stepped forward to carry the undertaking to its end, the feeling among them all was that a battle was necessary to be fought, and that the strength of this mighty Captain of our salvation was alone equal to the achievement of the victory.

Who is this that cometh from Edom, with dyed garments from Bozrah? this that is glorious in His apparel, travelling in the greatness of His strength? I that speak in righteousness, mighty to save. Wherefore art thou red in thine apparel, and thy garments like him that treadeth in the winevat? I have trodden the wine-press alone; and of the people there was none with me; for I will tread them in mine anger, and trample them in my fury; and their blood shall be sprinkled upon my garments, and I will stain all my raiment. For the day of vengeance is in mine heart, and the year of my redeemed is come. And I looked, and there was none to help; and I wondered that there was none to uphold; therefore mine own arm brought salvation unto me; and my fury, it upheld me. [Isaiah 63:1-5]

A way of redemption has been found out in the unsearchable riches of divine wisdom, and Christ is called the wisdom of God. But the same Christ is also called the power of God. In the mighty work of redemption He put forth a strength, and it is that strength that we are called to take hold upon. There was a wonderful strength in bearing the wrath that would have fallen on the millions and millions more of a guilty world. There was a strength that bore Him up under the agonies of the garden. There was a strength that supported Him under the hiding of His Father's countenance. There was a strength that upheld Him in the dark hour of the travail of His soul, and that one might think had well-nigh given way when He called out, "My God, my God, why hast Thou forsaken me?" (Luke 15:34). There was a strength that carried Him in triumph through the contest over Satan, when he buffeted Him with his temptations—a strength far greater than we know of in that mysterious struggle that He held with the powers of darkness, when Satan fell like lightning from heaven, and the captain of our salvation spoiled principalities and powers and made a show of them openly and triumphed over them. There was a strength in overcoming all the mighty difficulties that lay in the way between the sinner and God, in unbarring the gates of acceptance to a guilty world, in bringing truth and mercy to meet, and righteousness and peace to enter into fellowship—so that God might be just, while He is the justifier of him who believes in Jesus.

So much for the strength that is put forth in the work of man's redemption. But there is also strength put forth in the work of man's regeneration. Christ hath not only done a great work for us in making good our reconciliation with God. He further does a great work in us when He makes us like unto God.

But I have not time to dwell upon this last topic and must content myself with referring you to the following Scriptures: John 15:5; 2 Corinthians 12:9-10; Ephesians 1:19; 2:10; Philippians 4:13. The power that raised Jesus from the dead is the power that raises us from our death in trespasses and sins. The power that was put forth on creation is the power that makes us new creatures in Jesus Christ our Lord.

Neither have I time to make out a full demonstration of what is meant by laying hold of that strength. When you apply to a friend for some service, some relief from distress or difficulty, you may be said to lay hold of him. When you place firm reliance on both his ability and willingness to do you the service, you may well say that your hold is upon your friend—an expression that becomes all the more appropriate should he promise to do the needful good office, in which case your hold is not upon his power only, but upon his faithfulness.

It is even so with the promises of God in Christ Jesus; you have both a power and a promise to take hold of. If you believe that Christ is able to save to the uttermost all who come unto God through Him, and if you believe the honesty of His invitation to all who are weary and heavy-laden, that they might come unto Him and rest unto their souls, thus judging Him to be faithful who has promised, then indeed will you lay hold of Christ as the power of God unto salvation. According to the faith that has thus led you to fix upon the Savior, so will it be done unto you. To coninue in this faith is, in the language of Scripture, to hold fast your confidence and the rejoicing of your hope firm unto the end. Cast not away this confidence that hath great recompense of reward; or if you have not yet begun to place this confidence in the assurances of the gospel, lay hold of them now. They are addressed to each and to all of you. It is not a vague generality of which I am speaking. Let every man among you take up with Christ and trust in Him for yourself.

I am well aware that unless the Spirit reveal to

you, all I have said about Him will fall fruitless
upon your ears, and your hearts will remain as cold
and as heavy and as alienated as ever. Faith is His
gift, and it is not of ourselves. But the minister is at
his post when he puts the truth before you. You are
at your posts when you hearken diligently and have
a prayerful spirit of dependence on the giver of all
wisdom—that He will bless the word spoken and
make it reach your souls in the form of a salutary
and convincing application.

It is indeed wonderful—it is passing wonderful—
that there should be about us such an ungenerous
suspicion of our Father who is in heaven. It cannot
be sufficiently wondered at that all the ways in
which He sets Himself forth to us should have so
feeble an influence in the way of cheering us on to
a more delighted confidence. How shall we account
for it—that the barrier of unbelief should stand so
obstinately firm in spite of every attempt and every
remonstrance that the straitening should still continue (not the straitening of God toward us, for He
has said everything to woo us to put our trust in
Him—but the straitening of us toward God, whereby in the face of His every kind and exhilarating
declaration we persist in being cold and distant and
afraid of Him)?

I know not how far I may have succeeded as a
humble and unworthy instrument, in drawing aside
the veil that darkens the face of Him who sits on
the throne. But, oh, how imposing is the attitude,
and how altogether affecting is the argument with
which He comes forward to us in the text of this
day! It is not so much His saying that there is no
fury in Him; this He often tells us in other passages
of Scripture. The striking peculiarity of the words

123

now submitted to us is the way in which He would convince us how little interest He can have in our destruction and how far it is from His thoughts to aspire after the glory of such an achievement, as if He had said, "It would be nothing to Me to consume you all by the breath of My indignation. It would throw no illustration over Me to sweep away the whole strength of that rebellion that you have mustered up against Me. It would make no more to My glory than if I went through the thorns and briers and burned them before Me. This is not the battle I want to engage in; this is not the victory by which I seek to signalize myself. You mistake Me, you mistake Me, ye feeble children of men, if you think that I aspire after anything else with any one of you than that you should be prevailed on to come into My vineyard, lay hold of My strength, seek to make peace with Me, and you shall make peace with Me. The victory that My heart is set upon is not a victory over your persons—that is a victory that will easily be gotten in the great day of final reckoning over all who have refused My overtures, would none of My reproof, and have turned them away from My beseeching offers of reconciliation.

"In that great day of the power of Mine anger it will be seen how easy it is to accomplish such a victory as this. How rapidly the fire of My conflagration will involve the rebels who have opposed Me in that devouring flame from which they never, never can be extricated. How speedily the execution of the condemning sentence will run through the multitude who stand at the left hand of the avenging Judge."

Rest assured, ye men who are now hearing Me

and whom I freely invite to enter into the vineyard of God, that this is not the triumph that God is longing after. It is not a victory over your persons then of which He is at all ambitious. It is a victory over your wills now. It is that you do honor to His testimony by placing your reliance on it. It is that you accept of His kind and free assurances that He has no ill will to you. It is that you cast the whole burden of sullen fear and suspicion away from your hearts, and that now, even now, you enter into a fellowship of peace with the God whom you have offended.

Oh, be prevailed upon. I know that terror will not subdue you; I know that all the threatenings of the law will not reclaim you; I know that no direct process of pressing home the claims of God upon your obedience will ever compel you to the only obedience that is of any value in His estimation— even the willing obedience of the affections to a father whom you love.

But surely when He puts on in your sight the countenance of a father—when He speaks to you with the tenderness of a father—when He tries to woo you back to that house of His from which you have wandered and to persuade you of His goodwill, when He descends so far as to reason the matter and to tell you that He is no more seeking any glory from your destruction than He would seek glory from lighting into a blaze the thorns and the briers and burning them together—ah! my brethren, should it not look plain to the eye of faith how honest and sincere the God of your redemption is, who is thus bowing Himself down to the mention of such an argument! Do lay hold of it, be impressed by it, and cherish no longer any doubt of the goodwill of the Lord God, merciful and gracious. Let your faith work by love to Him who hath done so much and said so much to engage it, and let this love evince all the power of a commanding principle within you by urging your every footstep to the new obedience of new creatures in Jesus Christ your Lord.

Thus the two-fold benefit of the gospel will be realized by all who believe and obey that gospel. Reconciled to God by the death of His Son, regenerated by the power of that mighty and all-subduing Spirit who is at the giving of the Son, your salvation will be complete—washed and sanctified and justified in the name of the Lord Jesus and by the Spirit of our God.

ACCIDENTS, NOT PUNISHMENTS

Charles Haddon Spurgeon

(1834-1891)

Not only did Charles Haddon Spurgeon preach to vast audiences from the pulpit, but also to thousands all over the world through the printed page. His sermon on "Baptismal Regeneration" alone reached a circulation of well over 200,000 before his death.

In 1855 Spurgeon began what he called a "penny pulpit," when he printed one sermon a week. The popularity of these sermons grew until he had a weekly circulation of 25,000.

In January of 1888 Spurgeon published his two-thousandth sermon. On this occasion, he said to the people of the Metropolitan Tabernacle: "I have in my hand a sermon by which I set great store. It bears the initials D. L.; this is David Livingstone and is a sermon found inside of Dr. Livingstone's box. It is entitled, 'Accidents, Not Punishments,' No. 408, and on it is written, 'very good, D. L.' This was sent me by Mrs. Agnes Livingstone Bruce and is brown and worn, but I treasure it as a great relic, because that servant of God carried it with him and evidently carried it in his box."

It is said that Dr. Livingstone, while in England,

was a constant attendant upon the preaching of Mr.
Spurgeon, and so it is not to be wondered at that he
carried this sermon all over Africa in his strong box.

"Accidents, Not Punishments" was preached at
the Metropolitan Tabernacle on Sunday, September
8, 1861, shortly after a series of tragic accidents in
London that caused great alarm among the masses.

ACCIDENTS, NOT PUNISHMENTS

> *There were present at that season
> some that told him of the Galileans,
> whose blood Pilate had mingled with
> their sacrifices. And Jesus answering
> said unto them, Suppose ye that these
> Galileans were sinners above all the
> Galileans, because they suffered such
> things? I tell you, Nay: but, except ye
> repent, ye shall all likewise perish. Or
> those eighteen, upon whom the tower
> in Siloam fell, and slew them, think ye
> that they were sinners above all men
> that dwelt in Jerusalem? I tell you,
> Nay: but, except ye repent, ye shall all
> likewise perish* (Luke 13:1-5).

THE YEAR 1861 was a year of calamities. Just at
that season when man goes forth to reap the fruit of
his labors, when the harvest of the earth is ripe and
the barns are beginning to burst with the new
wheat, Death, the mighty reaper, has come forth to
cut down his harvest; full sheaves have been
gathered into his garner, the tomb, and terrible
have been the wailings that compose the harvest
hymn of death. In reading the newspapers during
the last two weeks, even the most stolid must have

been the subject of very painful feelings. Not only have there been catastrophes so alarming that the blood chills at their remembrance, but column after column of the paper has been devoted to calamities of a minor degree of horror, but which, when added together, are enough to astound the mind with the fearful amount of sudden death that has of late fallen on the sons of men.

We have had not only one accident for every day in the week, but two or three. We have not simply been stunned with the alarming noise of one terrific crash, but another, and another, and another, have followed upon each other's heels, like Job's messengers, till we have needed Job's patience and resignation to hear the dreadful tale of woes.

Now, such things as these have always happened in all ages of the world. Think not that this is a new thing. Do not dream, as some do, that this is the product of an overwrought civilization or of that modern and most wonderful discovery of steam. If the steam engine had never been known and if the railway had never been constructed, there would have been sudden deaths and terrible accidents notwithstanding.

In the old records in which our ancestors wrote down their accidents and calamities, we find that the old stagecoach yielded quite as heavy a booty to death as does the swiftly rushing train. There were gates to hades then as many as there are now and roads to death quite as steep and precipitous and traveled by quite as vast a multitude as in our present time. Do you doubt that?

Permit me to refer you to the chapter before you. Remember those eighteen upon whom the tower in Siloam fell. What if no collision crushed them; what if they were not destroyed by the ungovernable iron horse dragging them down from an embankment? Yet some badly built tower or some wall beaten by the tempest could fall upon eighteen at a time, and they might perish. Or worse than that, a despotic ruler, having the lives of men at his girdle like the keys of his palace, might suddenly fall upon worshipers in the Temple itself and mix their blood with the blood of the bullocks that they were then sacrificing to the God of heaven.

Do not think that this is an age in which God is dealing more severely with us than of old. Do not think that God's providence has become more lax than it was. There always were sudden deaths, and there always will be. There always were seasons when death's wolves hunted in hungry packs, and, probably, until the end of this dispensation, the last enemy will hold his periodic festivals and glut the worms with the flesh of men. Be not, therefore, cast down with any sudden fear, neither be troubled by these calamities. Go about your business, and if your avocations should call you to cross the field of death itself, do it, and do it bravely. God has not thrown up the reins of the world; He has not taken off His hand from the helm of the great ship, still

> *He everywhere hath sway,*
> *And all things serve His might;*
> *His every act pure blessing is,*
> *His path unsullied light.*

Only learn to trust Him, and you shall not be afraid of sudden fear. "Thy soul shall dwell at ease, and thy seed shall inherit the earth."

Our particular subject, however, is the use that

we ought to make of these fearful texts that God is writing in capital letters upon the history of the world. God hath spoken once, yea, twice; let it not be said that man regards it not. We have seen a glimmering of God's power; we have beheld something of the readiness with which He can destroy our fellow creatures. Let us "hear the rod and him that hath appointed it"; and in hearing it, let us do two things.

First, let us not be so foolish as to draw the conclusion of superstitious and ignorant persons, that conclusion that is hinted at in the text, that those who are thus destroyed by accident are sinners above all the sinners that are in the land.

And, second, let us draw the right and proper inference. Let us make practical use of all these events for our own personal improvement. Let us hear the voice of the Savior saying, "Except ye repent, ye shall all likewise perish."

First, then, *let us take heed that we do not draw the rash and hasty conclusion from terrible accidents, that those who suffer by them suffer on account of their sins.*

It has been most absurdly stated that those who travel on the first day of the week and meet with an accident ought to regard that accident as being a judgment from God because of their violation of the Christian's day of worship. It has been stated even by godly ministers that the late deplorable collision should be looked upon as an exceedingly wonderful and remarkable visitation of the wrath of God against those unhappy persons who happened to be in the Clayton tunnel.

Now I enter my solemn protest against such an inference, not in my own name, but in the name of

Him who is the Christian's master and the Christian's teacher. I say of those who were crushed in that tunnel, think ye that they were sinners above all sinners? "I tell you, Nay: but, except ye repent, ye shall all likewise perish."

I would not deny that there have sometimes been judgments of God upon particular persons for sin; sometimes, and I think but exceedingly rarely, such things have occurred. We have heard instances of men who have blasphemed God and defied Him to destroy them, who have fallen dead suddenly. In such cases, the punishment has so quickly followed the blasphemy that one could not help perceiving the hand of God in it. The man had wantonly asked for the judgment of God, his prayer was heard, and the judgment came.

And, beyond a doubt, there are what may be called natural judgments. You see a man ragged, poor, homeless; he has been profligate, he has been a drunkard, he has lost his character, and it is the just judgment of God upon him that he should be starving and that he should be an outcast among men. You see in the hospitals loathsome specimens of men and women foully diseased. God forbid that we should deny judgment of God upon licentiousness and ungodly lusts!

And the same may be said in many instances where there is so clear a link between the sin and the punishment that the blindest men may discern that God has made misery the child of sin. But in cases of accident such as that to which I refer and in cases of sudden and instant death, again I enter my earnest protest against the foolish and ridiculous idea that those who thus perish are sinners above all the sinners who survive unharmed.

Accidents, Not Punishments

Let me try to reason this matter out with Christian people; for there are some who will be horrified by what I have said. Those who are ready at perversions may even dream that I would apologize for the breach of the day of worship. I do no such thing; I do not extenuate the sin. I only testify and declare that accidents are not to be viewed as punishments for sin, for punishment belongs not to this world, but to the world to come. To all those who hastily look on every calamity as a judgment, I would speak in the earnest hope of setting them right.

Let me begin then by asking, Do you not see that what you say is not true? And that is the best of reasons why you should not say it. Does not your own experience and observation teach you that one event happens both to the righteous and to the wicked? It is true, the wicked man sometimes falls dead in the street; but has not the minister fallen dead in the pulpit? It is true that a pleasure boat, in which men were seeking their own pleasure on Sunday, has suddenly gone down. But is it not equally true that a ship that carried only godly men who were bound upon an excursion to preach the gospel has gone down too? The visible providence of God has no respect of persons; and a storm may gather around the "John Williams" missionary ship, quite as well as around a vessel filled with riotous sinners.

Why, do you not perceive that the providence of God has been, in fact, in its outward dealings rather harder upon the good than upon the bad? For, did not Paul say, as he looked upon the miseries of the righteous in his day, "If in this life only we have hope in Christ, we are of all men most miserable"?

The path of righteousness has often conducted men to the rack, to the prison, to the gallows, to the stake; while the road of sin has often led a man to empire, to dominion, and to high esteem among his fellows.

It is not true that in this world God does punish men for sin and reward them for their good deeds. Did not David say: "I have seen the wicked in great power, and spreading himself like a green bay tree"? Did not this perplex the psalmist for a little season until he went into the sanctuary of God, and then he understood their end?

Although your faith assures you that the ultimate result of providence will work out only good to the people of God, yet your life, though it be but a brief part of the divine drama of history, must have taught you that providence does not outwardly discriminate between the righteous and the wicked, that the righteous perish suddenly as well as the wicked, that the plague knows no difference between the sinner and the saint, and that the sword of war is alike pitiless to the sons of God and the sons of Belial. When God sends forth the scourge, it slays suddenly the innocent as well as the perverse and froward.

If your idea of an avenging and rewarding providence is not true, why should you talk as if it were? And why, if it is not correct as a general rule, should you suppose it is true in this one particular instance? Get the idea out of your head, for the gospel of God never needs you to believe an untruth.

But, second, there is another reason. The idea that whenever an accident occurs we are to look upon it as a judgment from God would make the providence of God to be a very shallow pool instead of a

great deep. Any child can understand the providence of God if it is true that when there is a railway accident it is because people travel on a Sunday. Take any child from the youngest class in the
Sunday school, and he will say, "Yes, I see that."
But then, if such a thing is providential, if it is a
providence that can be understood, manifestly it is
not the scriptural idea of providence, for in the
Scripture we are always taught that God's providence is "a great deep."

Even Ezekiel, who had the wing of the cherubim
and could fly aloft, when he saw the wheels that
were the great picture of the providence of God,
could only say the wheels were so high that they
were terrible and were full of eyes, so that he cried,
"O wheel!"

If a calamity were always the result of some sin,
providence would be as simple as that twice two
made four. It would be one of the first lessons that
a child might learn. But Scripture teaches us that
providence is a great depth in which the human
intellect may swim and dive, but it can neither find
a bottom nor a shore. If you and I pretend that we
can find out the reasons of providence and twist the
dispensations of God over our fingers, we only
prove our folly, but we do not prove that we have
begun to understand the ways of God. Why suppose for a moment there were some great perfor-
mance going on, and you should say, "Yes, I understand it," what a simpleton you would be!

Do you not know that the great transactions of
providence began six thousand years ago? You have
only stepped into this world for thirty or forty years
and have seen one actor on the stage, and you say
you understand it. You have only begun to know.

Only God knows the end from the beginning, only He understands what are the great results, what is the great reason for which the world was made and for which He permits both good and evil to occur. Think not that you know the ways of God. It is to degrade providence and to bring God down to the level of men when you pretend that you can understand those calamities and find out the secret designs of wisdom.

But next, do you not perceive that such an idea as this would encourage phariseeism? The people who were crushed to death, or scalded, or destroyed under the wheels of railway trains were worse sinners than we are? Very well, then what good people we must be; what excellent examples of virtue! We do not such things as they, and therefore God makes all things smooth for us. Inasmuch as we have traveled, some of us every day in the week, and yet have never been smashed to pieces, we may on this supposition rank ourselves with the favorites of deity. And then, would our safety be an argument for our being Christians? Our having traveled on a railway safely would be an argument that we were regenerate persons?

I have never read in the Scriptures, "We know that we have passed from death unto life, because we have traveled from London to Brighton safely twice a day." I have never found a verse that read like that. If it were true that the worst of sinners met with accidents, it would follow as a natural converse to that proposition that those who do not meet with accidents must be very good people, and what pharisaical notions we thus beget and foster! But I cannot indulge the folly for a moment.

As I look for a moment upon the poor mangled

bodies of those who have been killed so suddenly, my eyes fill with tears, but my heart does not boast nor my lips accuse. Far from me be the boastful cry, "God, I thank Thee that I am not as these men are!" Nay, nay, it is not the spirit of Christ, nor the spirit of Christianity.

Although we can thank God that we are preserved, we can say, "It is of thy mercy that we are not consumed," and we must ascribe it to His grace and to His grace alone. But we cannot suppose that there was any betterness in us, that we should be kept alive with death so near. It is only because He has had mercy, and has been very long-suffering toward us, not willing that we should perish but that we should come to repentance, that He has thus preserved us from going down to the grave and has kept us alive from death.

And then, permit me to remark that the supposition against which I am earnestly contending is a very cruel and unkind one. For if this were the case, that all persons who thus meet with their death in an extraordinary and terrible manner were greater sinners than the rest, would it not be a crushing blow to bereaved survivors? And is it not ungenerous on our part to indulge the idea, unless we are compelled by unanswerable reasons to accept it as an awful truth? I defy you to whisper it in the widow's ear. Go to her and say, "Your husband was a worse sinner than the rest of men, therefore he died." You have not brutality enough for that.

An unconscious infant who had never sinned, though doubtless an inheritor of Adam's fall, is found crushed amid the debris of the accident. Now think for a moment, what would be the infamous consequence of the supposition that those who perished were worse than others. You would have to say that this unconscious infant was a worse sinner than many in the dens of infamy whose lives are yet spared. Do you not perceive that the thing is radically false?

I might perhaps show the injustice of it by reminding you that it may one day turn upon your own head. Let it be your own case that you should meet with sudden death in such a way, are you willing to be adjudged to damnation on that account? Such an event may happen in the house of God.

Let me recall to my own and to your sorrowful recollection what occurred when once we met together. I can say with a pure heart we met for no object but to serve our God, and the minister had no aim in going to that place but that of gathering many to hear who otherwise would not have listened to his voice, and yet there were funerals as the result of a holy effort (for holy effort still we avow it to have been, and the aftersmile of God has proved it so). There were deaths among God's people. I was about to say I am glad it was with God's people rather than with others. A fearful fright took hold upon the congregation, and they fled. So if accidents are to be viewed as judgments, then is it a fair inference that we were sinning in being there, an insinuation that our consciences repudiate with scorn?

However, if that logic were true, it is as true against us as it is against others. And inasmuch as you would repel with indignation the accusation that any were wounded or hurt on account of sin, in being there to worship God, what you repel for yourself repel for others, and be no party to the accusation that is brought against those who have been destroyed during the past two weeks, that they perished on account of any great sin.

Here I anticipate the outcries of prudent and zealous persons who tremble for the ark of God and would touch it with Uzzah's hand. "Well," says one, "but we ought not to talk like this, for it is a very serviceable superstition, because there are many people who will be kept from traveling on a Sunday by the accident, and we ought to tell them, therefore, that those who perished, perished because they traveled on Sunday."

I would not tell a lie to save a soul, and that would be telling a lie, for it is not the fact. I would do anything to stop Sunday labor and sin, but I would not forge a falsehood even to do that. They might have perished on a Monday as well as on a Sunday. God gives no special immunity any day of the week, and accidents may occur as well at one time as at another. It is only a pious fraud when we seek thus to play upon the superstition of men to make capital for Christ. An honest Christian man who believes that the religion of Christ can take care of itself without telling falsehoods, scorns to do it. Those people did not perish because they traveled on a Sunday. Witness the fact that others perished on a Monday when they were on an errand of mercy.

I know not why God sent the accident. God forbid that we should offer our own reason when God has not given us His reason, but we are not allowed to make the superstition of men an instrument for advancing the glory of God.

Among Protestants there is a great deal of popery. I meet with people who uphold infant baptism on the plea, "Well, it is not doing any hurt, and there is a great deal of good meaning in it. It may do good, and even confirmation may be blessed to some people. Therefore do not let us speak against it."

I have nothing to do with whether the thing hurts or not. All I have to do with is whether it is right, whether it is scriptural, whether it is true, and if the truth does mischief, which is a supposition we can by no means allow, that mischief will not lie at our door. We have nothing to do but to speak the truth, even though the heavens should fall.

I say again, that any advancement of the gospel due to the superstition of men is a false advance, and it will recoil upon the people who use such an unhallowed weapon. We have a religion that appeals to man's judgment and common sense, and when we cannot get on with that, I scorn that we should proceed by any other means. If there be any person who should harden his heart and say, "Well, I am as safe on one day as another," which is quite true, I must say to him, "The sin of your making such a use as this of a truth must lie at your own door, not at mine.

"But if I could keep you from violating the Christian's day of rest by putting before you a superstitious hypothesis, I would not do it, because I feel that though I might keep you from that one sin a little time, you would grow too intelligent to be duped by me, and then you would come to look upon me as a priest who had played upon your fears instead of appealing to your judgment."

It is time for us to know that our Christianity is not a weak, shivering thing that appeals to the petty superstitious fears of ignorant and darkened minds. It is a manly thing, loving the light and needing no sanctified frauds for its defense. Turn your light upon us, and let it glare into our eyes. We are not afraid. Truth is mighty and it can prevail. If it cannot prevail in the daylight, we have no wish that the sun should set to give it an opportunity. I believe that much infidelity has sprung from the very natural desire of some Christian people to make use of common mistakes. "Oh," they have said, "this popular error is a very good one, it keeps people right; let us perpetuate the mistake, for it evidently does good." And then, when the mistake has been found out, infidels have said, "You see now these Christian people are found out in their tricks."

Let us have no tricks; let us not talk to men as though they were little children and could be frightened by tales of ghosts and witches. The fact is, that this is not the time of retribution, and it is worse than idle for us to teach that it is so.

And now, do you not perceive that the unchristian and unscriptural supposition, that when men suddenly meet with death it is the result of sin, robs Christianity of one of its noblest arguments for the immortality of the soul? We assert daily, with Scripture for our warrant, that God is just; and inasmuch as He is just, He must punish sin and reward the righteous. Manifestly He does not do it in this world.

I have plainly shown that in this world, one event happens to both; that the righteous man is poor as well as the wicked and that he dies suddenly as well as the most graceless.

The inference is natural and clear that there must be a next world in which these things must be righted. If there is a God, He must be just; and if He is just, He must punish sin; and since He does not do it in this world, there must be another state in which men shall receive the due reward of their works. They that have sown to the flesh shall of the flesh reap corruption, while they that have sown to the Spirit shall of the Spirit reap life everlasting. Make this world the reaping place, and you have taken the sting out of sin.

"Oh," say the sinners, "if the sorrows men endure here are all the punishment they will have, we will sin greedily!" Say to them, "No; this is not the world of punishment, but the world of probation. It is not the court of justice, but the land of mercy. It is not the prison of terror, but the house of long-suffering," and you have opened before their eyes the gates of the future. You have set the judgment throne before their eyes. You have reminded them of "Come, ye blessed," and "Depart, ye cursed." You have a more reasonable, not to say a more scriptural, ground of appeal to their consciences and to their hearts.

I have thus spoken with the view of correcting the idea that is too current among the ungodly that we as Christians hold every calamity to be a judgment. We do not! We do not believe that those eighteen upon whom the tower in Siloam fell were sinners above all the sinners that were in Jerusalem.

Now to our second point. *What use, then, ought we to make of this voice of God as heard amid the shrieks and groans of dying men?* Two uses: first, inquiry; and second, warning.

The first inquiry we should put to ourselves is this: "Why may not I very soon and suddenly be cut off? Have I a lease on my life? Have I any special guardianship that insures me that I shall not suddenly pass the portals of the tomb? Have I received a charter of longevity? Have I been covered with such a coat of armor that I am invulnerable to the arrows of death? Why am not I to die?"

And the next question it should suggest is this: "Am not I as great a sinner as those who died? Are there not in me sins against the Lord my God? If in outward sin others have excelled me, are not the thoughts of my heart evil? Does not the same law that curses them curse me? I have not continued in all the things that are written in the book of the law to do them. It is as impossible that I should be saved by my works as that they should be. Am not I under the law as well as they by nature, and therefore am not I as well as they under the curse?

"Instead of thinking of the sins of others, which would make me proud, I should think of my own, which will make me humble. Instead of speculating upon their guilt, which is no business of mine, I should turn my eyes within and think on my own transgression, for which I must personally answer before the Most High God.

Then the next question is, "Have I repented of my sin?" I need not inquire whether they have or not. Have I? Since I am liable to the same calamity, am I prepared to meet it?

Have I felt, through the Holy Spirit's convincing power, the blackness and depravity of my heart? Have I been led to confess before God that I deserve His wrath, and that His displeasure, if it light on me, will be my just due? Do I hate sin? Have I learned to abhor it? Have I, through the Holy Spirit, turned away from it as from a deadly poison, and do I seek now to honor Christ my Master? Am I washed in His blood? Do I bear His likeness? Do I reflect His character? Do I seek to live to His praise?

For if not, I am in as great danger as they were, and may be cut off quite as suddenly, and then where am I? I will not ask where are they? And then again, instead of prying into the future destiny of those unhappy men and women, how much better to inquire into our own destiny and our own state!

What am I? my soul awake,
And an impartial survey take.

Am I prepared to die? If now the gates of hell should be opened, shall I enter there? If now beneath me the wide jaws of death should gape, am I prepared with confidence to walk through the midst of them, fearing no evil, because God is with me?

That is the proper use to make of accidents. That is the wisest way to apply the judgments of God to our own selves and to our own condition. God has spoken to every man in London during these last two weeks. He has spoken to me, He has spoken to you, men, women, and children. God's voice has rung out of the dark tunnel, has spoken from the sunset and from the glaring bonfire around which lay the corpses of men and women, and He has said to you, "Be ye also ready, for in such an hour as ye think not, the Son of man cometh." I hope it may set you to inquiring, "Am I prepared? Am I ready? Am I willing now to face my judge and hear the sentence pronounced upon my soul?"

When we have used this for inquiry, let me remind you that we ought to use it also for warning. "Ye shall all likewise perish." "No," says one, "not likewise. We shall not all be crushed; many of us

144

will die in our beds. We shall not all be burned; many of us will calmly close our eyes."

But the text says, "Ye shall all likewise perish." And let me remind you that some of you may perish in the same manner. You have no reason to believe that you may not also be cut off suddenly while walking the streets. You may fall dead while eating your meals. How many have perished with the staff of life in their hands! You may be in your bed, and your bed shall suddenly be made your tomb. You may be strong, hale, hearty, and either by an accident or by the stoppage of the circulation of your blood, you shall be suddenly hurried before your God. May sudden death to you be sudden glory!

But this may happen to some of us, that in the same sudden manner as others have died, so shall we. But lately in America, while preaching the Word, a brother laid down his body and his charge at once. You will remember the death of Dr. Beaumont, who closed his eyes to earth while proclaiming the gospel of Christ. And I remember the death of a minister in this country, who had just given out the verse,

> Father, I long, faint to see
> The place of Thine abode;
> I'd leave Thine earthly courts and flee
> Up to Thy house, my God,

when it pleased God to grant him the desire of his heart, and he appeared before the King in His beauty. Why, then, may not such a sudden death happen to you and to me?

But it is quite certain that, let death come when it

145

may, there are some few respects in which it will come to us in just the same manner as it has to those who have so lately been hurried away. First, it will come quite as surely. They could not, travel as fast as they would, escape from the pursuer. They could not, journey where they may, from home or to home, escape the shaft when the time had come. And so shall we perish. Just as certainly as death has set its seal upon the corpses that are now covered with the sod, so certainly shall it set its seal on us (unless the Lord should come before), for "it is appointed unto men once to die, but after this the judgment" (Hebrews 9:27). There is no discharge in this way; there is no escape for any individual by any bypath; there is no bridge over this river; there is no ferryboat by which we may cross this Jordan dry-shod.

Into thy chill depths, O river, each one of us must descend; in thy cold stream, our blood must be frozen; and beneath thy foaming billows our head must sink. We, too, must surely die. "Trite," you say, "and commonplace"; and death is commonplace, but it happens only once to us.

God grant that once dying may perpetually be in our minds till we die daily and find it not hard work to die at the last.

Well, then, as death comes both to them and to us surely, so will it come both to them and to us most potently and irresistibly. When death surprised them, then what help had they? A child's card house was not more easily crushed than those ponderous coaches. What could they do to help one another? They are sitting talking side by side. A scream is heard, and ere a second cry can be uttered, they are crushed and mangled.

Accidents, Not Punishments

The husband may seek to extricate his wife, but heavy timbers have covered her body. He can only find at last her poor head, and she is dead, and he sorrowfully takes his place by her side, and puts his hand upon her brow, until it is stone cold; and though he has seen one and another plucked with broken bones from the midst of the ruined mass, he must leave her body there. His children are motherless, and he himself is robbed of the partner of his bosom. They could not resist; they might do what they could, but as soon as the moment came, on they went, and death or broken bones was the result.

So with you and me; bribe the physician with the largest fee, but he could not put fresh blood into your veins; pay him in masses of gold, but he could not make the pulse give another throb. Death, irresistible conqueror of men, there is none that can stand against thee; thy word is law, thy will is destiny! So shall it come to us as it did to them; it shall come with power, and none of us can resist.

When it came to them, it came instantly, and would not brook delay. So will it come to us. We may have longer notice than they, but when the hour has struck there shall be no postponing it. Gather up thy feet in thy bed, O patriarch, for thou must die and not live! Give the last kiss to thy wife, thou veteran soldier of the cross; put thy hands upon thy children's heads and give them the dying benediction, for all thy prayers cannot lengthen out thy life, and all of thy tears cannot add a drop to the dry wellspring of thy being. Thou must go; the Master sendeth for thee, and He brooks no delay. Nay, though thy whole family should be ready to sacrifice their lives to buy thee but an hour of respite, it must not be.

147

Though a nation should be a holocaust, a willing sacrifice, to give its sovereign another week in addition to his reign, yet it must not be. Though the whole flock should willingly consent to tread the dark vaults of the tomb to let their pastor's life be spared but for another year, it must not be. Death will have no delay; the time is up, the clock has struck, the sand has run out, and as certainly as they died when their time was come, in the field by sudden accident, so certainly must we.

And then, again, let us remember that death will come to us as it did to them, with terrors. Not with the crash of broken timbers, perhaps; not with the darkness of the tunnel; not with the smoke and the steam; not with the shrieks of women and groans of dying men, but yet with terrors. For meet death where we may, if we are not in Christ, and if the shepherd's rod and staff do not comfort us, to die must be an awful and tremendous thing.

Yes, in thy body, O sinner, with downy pillows beneath thy head, and a wife's tender arm to bear thee up, and a tender hand to wipe thy clammy sweat, thou wilt find it awful work to face the monster and feel his sting and enter into his dread dominions. It is awful work at any time and at every time, under the best and most propitious circumstances, for a man to die unprepared.

And now I would send you away with this one thought. We are dying creatures, not living creatures, and we shall soon be gone. Perhaps as here I stand and talk of these mysterious things, soon shall this hand be stretched and dumb the mouth that lisps the faltering strain.

Power supreme, O everlasting King, come when Thou mayest. Mayest Thou ne'er intrude upon an ill-spent hour; but find me wrapped in meditation high, hymning my great Creator; doing works of mercy to the poor and needy ones; or bearing in my arms the poor and weary of the flock; or solacing the disconsolate; or blowing the blast of the gospel trumpet in the ears of the deaf and perishing souls! Then come when Thou wilt, if Thou art with me in life, I shall not fear to meet Thee in death. But, oh, let my soul be ready with her wedding garment, with her lamp trimmed and her light burning, ready to see her Master and enter into the joy of her Lord!

Souls, you know the way of salvation. You have heard it often; hear it yet again. "He that believeth on the Son hath everlasting life" (John 3:36). "He that believeth and is baptized shall be saved; but he that believeth not shall be damned" (Mark 16:16). Believe with your heart, and with your mouth make confession. May the Holy Spirit give you grace to do both. And then you may say,

Come, death, and some celestial band.
To bear my soul away!

A LIVING STONE

Handley C. G. Moule

(1841-1920)

After preaching in Trinity Church of Cambridge for twenty-one years (1880-1901), Handley C. G. Moule was appointed Bishop of Durham, succeeding Bishop Westcott.

By privilege, the bishops of Durham can claim to support the sovereign on his right hand at the coronation. In 1902, Moule stood at the right hand of King Edward VII, during the coronation in Westminster Abbey and at the side of King George V in 1911.

On April 18, 1920, Moule was summoned to preach in the private chapel at Windsor before the king and queen. That was his last sermon. He preached on "A Living Stone," taking his text from 1 Peter 2:4-5. For several days he had been in great pain from sciatica and was wheeled from York Tower to the drawing room to await the arrival of the king and queen. On Sunday morning he was taken to the private chapel, and although he looked very pale and tired it is said that he spoke with a stronger voice than usual.

The next day Moule returned to the home of his brother at Cambridge, where he remained until his death on May 8, 1920.

Handley C. G. Moule

A LIVING STONE

*To whom [him] coming, as unto a
living stone . . . ye also, as lively [liv-
ing] stones, are built up* (1 Peter 2:4-5).

HERE, IN A SENTENCE, a great Christian tells us
the vital secret for the development of Christian
character. The sentence is on one hand a fragment
of the holy Scriptures, nothing less than a word of
God, suggested and guided from above. (On the
other hand, it finds utterance through a man altogether human, who speaks out of the moving depths
of convictions and experiences profoundly personal.)

He is the Peter of the Galilean lake, of the garden
of the agony, of the courtyard of the high priest. He
bears in him a natural heart capable of the extremes
of devotion and of weakness, this Peter, whom his
Lord so wonderfully lifted out of the swellings and
the panics of ungoverned impulse into the balanced
power of a large and loving wisdom; out of the self-
reliance that let him drop into the horror of his
denials up to a strength of faith, that is to say of a
reliant use of his Savior as his victory, that made
him, through long years of toil and peril, crowned
with the awful glory of his martyr-cross, a Peter
indeed, a Cephas, a man of living rock.

It is he who speaks here in this wonderful writing, as beautiful in diction as it is divine in matter,
his first epistle. He addresses his disciples of the
scattered Asian missions but also ourselves today.
For these apostolic letters, unique vehicles of revelation, informal, friendly, shaped and phrased pre-
cisely in the form and dialect of the common cor-
respondence of their time, are the Word of God,

which abides forever, contemporary with every
date.

The writer is telling those Asiatics then, and ourselves now, what is the formative power for the full
Christian life, the complete Christian character in
action, strong but tender, humble but prevailing,
immovable in principle and purpose, yet open as
the air to all pure sympathies and all generous
service.

(For such a growth the type must be the Christ,
the perfect man, the more than realization in manhood of its supreme ideal of blended power and
love.)Yet more, the Christ must be the life, the victory of His followers. The dynamic behind their
ethic, their power alike to achieve and to serve, it is
their Lord, their Savior, personal and present, ac-
cessible to their spirits' use.

Christ first, then, Peter denotes and describes. He
is the Living Stone. This is a pregnant designation.
And it is, I think, given to our Master only here. We
find Him often figured as the Rock, the Stone of
the corner. We find Him revealed often as the very
Life, "Christ which is our life." Here the two ideas
converge into one magnificent and gracious mystery—the Living Stone.

The Stone comes first to our thought. The word
suggests all that is massive, ponderous, steadfast.
The reference, no doubt, touches specially the
angulare fundamentum,the vast block of the corner,
clamping wall into wall as they meet beside it and
upon it. This is as parable for all that is inflexible,
for truth, changeless in everlasting rectitude, able
almightily to resist and to sustain.

Before us in this great word is revealed the Christ
as the mighty one in the moral battle, living always

as we see Him in the gospels, at the utmost height of a more than heroic virtue. He is never for a moment doubtful of Himself, never afraid of any foe, till in the last tremendous ordeal He not only endures the cross, with a transcendent firmness always more wonderful as we ponder it, but despises the shame, with a scorn such as only the sublimest spirit could pour upon degrading wrong.

And He, the Stone, is the same today and forever in this moral might of His. Cliffs and crags may suggest His fixity, yet all the while what are they beside it but fleeting shadows, unsubstantial dreams?

But, then, on the other hand this Christ, in Peter's faith, is the Stone that lives. Here, as often in the vivid richness of the Bible, the imagery bursts the bounds of nature. It gives us a rock instinct with a glowing consciousness of love.

This mass of power, "foursquare to opposition," we look at again. He, the Stone, has heart, and eyes, and arms, and voice. He lives, all over and all through; His life pours itself out to the refugee beneath Him in tenderness, as when a mother comforteth; in a compassion that does not so much condescend as share; in a matchless fellowship with weakness, with sorrow, with remorse; in an embracing fondness over the little child; in a magnetic pardoning kindness for the damaged wanderer of the street; in that skill of the experienced sufferer that can touch into joy the broken heart.

Such, somewhat such (for weak is this effort at a recollection of His glories) is the Living Stone. Every detail is familiar to our minds. But we never lose by a deliberate reassertion to the heart of the wonders of the Christian creed, built as that creed is out of the wealth of the gospel fact of Christ.

For myself, let me own it, as a long life including a Christian ministry of more than fifty years wears to its close, the soul of the messenger is always more possessed by the glory of the message. And that message, with an ever stronger emphasis, sums itself up for the servant in the perfections of the Master, the unsearchable riches of the Christ.

But the apostle has not finished. He has more to say, and of the same kind. The Living Stone is one, absolutely and by itself. But there are many living stones. We have looked at the supreme character of the Christ of God, upon the greatness that glows with goodness, upon the rock that beats with an eternal love. Well, that character, we gather here, is in some sort and measure communicable. For the apostle has hardly named the Living Stone, elect and precious, before his pen, almost in the same stroke, writes down the words, "Ye also, as living stones."

The secret of the wonderful possibility thus indicated we will think of later. For the moment let us give the fact a deliberate recollection. A man, a mortal man, a sinful man, the being not of romance but of today, called to live, not in some fancied environment where there is leisure to be good, but in the thick of common intercourse in the complex of modern claims and duties—they may be the highest, they may be what seem the least of all— can be, and can continue to the last to be, a living stone. *We are living Stones*

Take the two elements of the metaphor in turn, as we took them just now with reference to the Lord. The disciple can be in some measure, like his Master, a stone, a rock. He can, out of whatever *a* weakness, be made strong for God. Be his natural inconstancy what it may, he can become a stone of strength, solid, "sincere on virtue's side," steadfast with a persistency of dutiful conduct that stays and does not fail in the march of life. Conscience and will can somehow converge and embrace each other in Him; and the resultant amalgam is a character that invites reliance and fortifies, in all who touch it, every right resolve.

Then the man can be a living stone, as His Lord the Rock is living. He is not too good (if such a goodness could exist, which it cannot) to be alive with generous lovingkindness; with human sympathies and affections; with a warm and unselfish will to live at the service of others.

He is no such unhappy being as to dream of saying to another, or of thinking about another, "I am holier than thou." Out of nature he has indeed been taken into grace. But then grace, that is to say, God working in his will, has only led him up into a truer and nobler naturalness. He is natural, with every instinct of human kindness. He is faithful to right and to duty, if need be even to death. And he is only the more alive with instinctive aptitudes, warmed and vivified in the love of God, for his part in the dear fellowship of human life.

It is a radiant ideal, assuredly, this human personality, true with a stonelike moral firmness, but warm and companionable all the while. Here is a scholar versed in the Christian grammar of the pronouns, who recites them in an order nobler than that of the school book. The first Person for Him is *He*, the Lord supreme. The second is *You*, the other, the neighbor, the being in need of his help, light, and cheer. The third person is *I*, the self, left anywhere, left last, left out.

A Living Stone

And this ideal is no mere glory in the clouds, no dream of the poet, no theory of the Utopian moralist. It is just the Christian character in its sober truth, that character that sprung at once, full grown, from the creative power of Calvary and Pentecost, from the fact of a self-sacrificing God Incarnate and the gift of His Spirit in the spirits of His disciples.

Deep in the vast structure of the proof of Christianity lies that swift moral creation, that instant issue, from a revelation of transcendent wonders, from incarnation, sacrificial death of the Incarnate, and then His resurrection and His glory, of a type of human life so magnificently sober and beneficent.

Your life is hid with Christ in God; you are joined to the Lord; you have fellowship with the Father and the Son; honor all men, owe no man anything, study to be quiet, do your own business, eat your own bread, abstain from every form of evil, be not weary in well-doing.

No fanatical illusion could ever be the root of such a tree of life, with its wholesome fruit and its healing leaves. The mystery of our faith comes from above the heavens. But its history is as solid as the earth on which it was wrought out. And this summer daylight of its moral results, its production of this ordered character of invincible but loving virtue, sets a seal all its own to the history of the wonders from which it sprung.

No, this character is indeed no dream. It was a fact of experience for those disciples of Peter, those men and women lately steeped in surroundings of Levantine vice. They were actually living stones in the judgment of the apostle. It was a fact two generations later, in the view of a keen outside observer, the non-Christian Aristides, in his Appeal (rediscovered in our time) to the emperor to stay the persecutions. For the moral of the Christians' life, he says, personal, domestic, social, commerical, is what the world has never seen before, and the world must hail it now as its best hope. Aye, and it has been a fact all down the centuries; it is a fact today.

Shall I venture upon a personal reminiscence? May I touch with reverent hand the death and life of a Cambridge contemporary of my own? He died at twenty-two, of typhoid fever, in a Swiss hotel. His dearest ones, parents and sisters, were around him. But he, their ardent lover, now knew them no more; no gleam of recognition came. Then someone said, "Do you know Jesus?" "Jesus!" was the instant answer. "I know Him, and He knows me; I love Him, and He loves me." So he died.

But how had he lived? He had been destined by his father for the army, and after Cheltenham he passed for a three years' course to a military academy. It was a fine school of the soldier's science. But at that time its moral discipline was slack, and the common life was very evil. Arthur Elliott was no man of steel by nature; and he entered on his years as a cadet little aware of their impending temptations.

But just as his residence began, he came under the spiritual spell of a woman as wise and large-hearted as she was saintly, Catherine Marsh, of blessed memory. The lad, as the gracious prophetess pointed him to the Christ, rose as it were to be a living stone. Never deformed by the spirit of the Pharisee, ready always for fellowship and friendship, he lived his life there with unswerving steadfastness; true, in the strength of his adored and trusted Redeemer, absolutely true to duty and to virtue. His brain was sound and keen. I have his portrait on my wall; he sits in his cadet's uniform, the gold medal on the table by him, the sword of honor across his knees.

But he left at last, forbidden by delicacy of health to fulfill his promise in arms, and allowed by his father to enter Cambridge and satisfy the cherished hope of ordination, he left the military school with a distinction transcendently higher than swords and medals. Vice in that college (so I know from old men once his comrades there) was out of fashion; the old evils had come to be bad form.

The living stone had so stood and so lived that it developed a magnetic influence. The weaker men of good intent drew to him at once as their strength and stay; the circle grew, and the place was another place.

So lived and so died a living stone. His face, nobly pure, gently strong, looks often in upon my soul. *Frater, ave atque vale!* Brother, all hail! I thank God I ever saw thee, and felt, however faintly, yet really, the power of the living stone in thee.

If the single stones of the spiritual quarry are such, what cannot the structure be? Ye are builded up. What must it not mean for good, for virtue, for the penetration of the mass of human life, not least in these days of man's vast bewilderment, with its one true cleansing, and ordering, and ennobling secret, the fear of God, that is to say, love upon its knees before the Eternal Truth and Love, when living stone meets living stone, when life meets life, when strength meets strength, in the co-operant force of a membership one of another, with hearts and hands united in the faith, and love, and blissful hope of Jesus Christ our Lord!

We remember, as we close, that to secure this coherent and co-operant power in our common life, as well as to secure the Christian character in the man, there is one secret, only one. That secret is a living contact with the archetypal living stone. It is nothing less than the Christ in divinely magnetic contact with us men. There, from the first even to the last, resides the transforming talisman. Perpetual, persistent touch with Him, in all and every way, in converse with Him through prayer, through Scripture, through sacrament, through recollection, through loyal service of Him in others, this is the vital requisite.

The Greek of Peter, by the verbal form of the word we render "coming," implies this persistency; "coming and coming again"; aye, as our breathing comes, and the pulses of our blood. For pardon, for purity, for spirit-power, we must be ceaseless applicants to the Christ; we must touch always the Living Stone, as old Antaeus in the legend touched his mother earth and was invincible again.

So, true in His truth, strong in His strength, shall we be and abide His living stones, moral results of Him.

Moody Press, a ministry of the Moody Bible Institute, is designed for education, evangelization and edification. If we may assist you in knowing more about Christ and the Christian life, please write us without obligation to: Moody Press, c/o MLM, Chicago, Illinois 60610.